ROOM 24

"I'm thrilled to have this book from Katie Prejean! She is a blessing for the Church and a definite standout among Catholic speakers today. Her passion for Christ and the work of his Church is contagious and this book is brimming with her inspirational vision and practical advice."

Chris Stefanick
Founder and President of Real Life Catholic

"Whether you are a new or a seasoned pastoral minister or teacher, read *Room 24: Adventures of a New Evangelist*! You will appreciate Katie Prejean's blend of humor and storytelling, the way she illustrates theological and pastoral insights through her lived experiences with young people, and the very real challenges and questions that they pose. You will find yourself recalling your own stories of starting out in ministry. You may even remember why you chose to do it in the first place. What a pleasure to have this book!"

Bob McCarty
Executive Director
National Federation for Catholic Youth Ministry

"What I love about this book is how Katie reminds us that evangelizing isn't about filling heads with more information; it's about encountering others in an authentic relationship that points them and you to the saving love of Christ."

Christopher Wesley
Author of *Rebuilding Youth Ministry*

"Katie Prejean has created a lively, engaging, and personal chronicle that serves as a point of departure for an insightful reflection on the New Evangelization. Her experiences will benefit those who seek to bring the message of Christ and his Church to others in a contemporary context."

Most Rev. Glen John Provost
Bishop of Lake Charles

"*Room 24* will make you laugh, give you pause for reflection, have you remembering all your crazy moments in ministry, and give you inspiration to deal with the ones you face now. It's good to remember that in ministry, we are all in it together, and we all have a stake in what goes on in room 24."

Jackie Francois Angel
Catholic speaker, worship leader, and recording artist

ROOM 24

ADVENTURES OF A NEW EVANGELIST

KATIE PREJEAN

Ave Maria Press AVE Notre Dame, Indiana

Founded in 1865, Ave Maria Press is a ministry of the United States Province of Holy
Cross.

www.avemariapress.com

Paperback: ISBN-13 978-1-59471-649-2

E-book: ISBN-13 978-1-59471-650-8

Cover image © Thinkstock.

Cover and text design by Katherine J. Ross.

Printed and bound in the United States of America.

Library of Congress Cataloging-in-Publication Data
Names: Prejean, Katie.
Title: Room 24 : adventures of a new evangelist / Katie Prejean.
Other titles: Room twenty-four
Description: Notre Dame, Indiana : Ave Maria Press, Inc., 2016. | Includes
    bibliographical references.
Identifiers: LCCN 2015037934 | ISBN 9781594716492 | ISBN 1594716498
Subjects: LCSH: Evangelistic work--Catholic Church. | Witness bearing
    (Christianity)--Catholic Church.
Classification: LCC BX2347.4 .P74 2016 | DDC 282.092--dc23
LC record available at http://lccn.loc.gov/2015037934

To my parents, who were my first and best teachers.

To my teachers, who taught me the immense joy of being a student.

To my students, from whom I have learned more than I could ever teach.

CONTENTS

Foreword by Mike Patin ix

Preface.. xi

1. What Can't You Live Without? 1

2. Where Jesus Is Lord 17

3. Seventy-Two Percent Compatible 25

4. Joy Down in the Heart..39

5. Eat, Teach, Sleep. Repeat. 53

6. Cute Shoes..67

7. The Miracle of Room 24 81

8. From the Fear...97

9. Stump Miss Prejean! 111

10. Avoiding the Greatest Tragedy 127

Acknowledgments...137

FOREWORD

The people of our day are more impressed by witnesses than by teachers, and if they listen to these, it is also because they bear witness.
—Pope Paul VI

In September 2005, shortly after Hurricane Rita had ravaged much of southwest Louisiana, I gave the keynote address at a simplified youth conference in the Diocese of Lake Charles. It was a challenging time for our community, and I struggled with what to say. I wanted something moving, profound, and eloquent to say to a group that needed words of hope. Preceding me was a witness talk by one of the teen participants. She was a gangly, red-headed high school student who spoke with energy and passion and had me mesmerized, even reticent to follow her.

That was my first encounter with Katie Prejean. She reminds me that I told her then that she would be popular on the Catholic speaking circuit one day. That was not prophetic; it was merely obvious that this young woman had gifts of communication, conviction, and charisma.

Those three things—great communication skills, conviction, and charisma—define the public face of this unique young woman who is causing ripples by her message, her style, and her joy in speaking and teaching, in evangelizing and catechizing, in discipling and forming teens in the Catholic faith today.

Katie is hungry for knowledge—in theology, in pedagogy, in speaking style, in being effective as a minister and as a daughter of God. She works hard at the craft of teaching, never content to coast or call in a lesson. She wants students to feel the energy and experience the passion she has for Jesus Christ, his Gospel, and the Catholic Church.

What impresses me most about this book is how Katie shows vulnerability, openness, and humility in the day-to-day adventure of being a modern day missionary, sharing with both neophytes and grizzled veterans her passion and her learnings. Her youth is deceptive; she is accruing a great amount of wisdom the old-fashioned way—earning it, by trial and error, and then willingly sharing it with the rest of us.

Reading these pages, I believe you will laugh, think, and agree (or not), but you will not stand on the sidelines. Katie is too good a teacher *not* to evoke some response from us. In that way, she imitates the Master Teacher, whom we all serve. I think the highest compliment I can give is to confess that I would very much like to be a student in Room 24.

Mike Patin
Catholic speaker and author

PREFACE

In the spring of 2012, I was offered a job teaching ninth-grade theology at the high school from which I had graduated five years earlier. The night before I walked back into the halls of that school—this time as a faculty member, and not a student in my pleated plaid skirt, I posted this Facebook status:

> *Tuesday, August 14, 2012*
> Tomorrow is my first day as a teacher at St. Louis Catholic High School. There are far too many thoughts flooding my brain right now, so I'll just write that I'm nervous, pumped, honored to have this chance, and scared to make a mistake all at the same time. I hope they like me! Pray for me!

Armed with a BA in theology, an enthusiasm for talking about all things Catholic, and no formal teacher training, I began each class that day with an impassioned and detailed speech about the nature of theology and why the study of God was the study of the most real thing in the universe. I was telling jokes, I was quoting saints, I was explaining how the class was going to be structured, and I was doing it all with an incredible amount of enthusiasm. I was Kobe Bryant, Room 24 was my court, and each line I was giving was a three-point shot made from center court. Nothin' but Truth . . . swoosh! As far as I was concerned, there was no way these fourteen-year-olds weren't going to love Jesus and theology as much as I did by the end of the school year.

Then a student raised his hand. Here it was—the first student question of the year. What would he ask? Would he want to know my favorite book? Was he going to tell me my motivational explanation of the two-page syllabus was inspiring him to become a priest? This was it! This was *the* critical moment, which could determine how my students would think of me for months to come.

> *Student*: Ummm, Miss Prejean, is that coffee in your cup?
>
> *Me*: Yeah, it is. Why do you ask?
>
> *Student*: Is that why you're so perky?
>
> *Me*: Well that, but also my excitement about this class!
>
> *Student*: Oh. Well, you might want to just blame the coffee, because otherwise we're gonna think you're a really big Catholic nerd.

I went home after school that day, collapsed on my couch, and posted another status.

> *Wednesday, August 15, 2012*
> Teaching is hard. Freshmen are mean. I am tired.

The second day of teaching was just as hard, and exhilarating, as the first. So were the third, fourth, fifth, and sixth days. Come to think of it, the entire first month was pretty exhausting, mentally and physically. The first year was mostly a blur of confusion and chaos with a few moments of success smattered throughout. At the very least, I knew the material I had taught my students was substantive, and I knew that at least a handful of them could tell me a few things about the Catholic faith. There was a steep learning curve for me that first year, and the countless lessons I learned then, and in the years since, have made me a better educator and a better person.

On the last day of school that first year of teaching, after bidding my students farewell for the much-needed summer break, I posted this:

> *Friday, May 24, 2013*
> I've learned three things this year . . .
> 1. Fake it 'til you make it
> 2. Trust Jesus
> 3. Love them

Spending five days a week in Room 24 with a bunch of fourteen-year-olds has had a profound impact on who I am, what I believe, and how I worship. Teachers educate their students, forming their minds and we hope, their lives. I have found, though, that my students have taught me just as much as I have taught them. My students have made me laugh, cry, sing (poorly, I might add), yell, study, pray, and dance (again, quite poorly). They have tested the limits of my faith, criticized and complimented my entire wardrobe, challenged me to become healthier, and pestered me about my personal life (to the point of creating dating profiles on my behalf!). I have shared my knowledge with them, and in turn, they have shared their lives with me. My students, and the parents who have sent them to my school, have given me the most beautiful gift of all: the chance to show them the face of Christ, being his hands and feet to them each day we are together in Room 24. My job is to teach them, but I have been privileged to become a student of my own students and to learn more from them about how to know, love, and serve Jesus than any theology course or textbook could ever have taught me.

This book is not a memoir. I don't think I'm old enough to have a memoir. This book is also not a definitive guide on how to teach religion to high school students, although any teachers reading it may find a few tips. This book is not a detailed outline on what to do as a rookie teacher—in fact it's a perfect example of what not to do in the first few years. Rather, this book is a collection of stories and quotes from Room 24, each one providing a lesson in how to live life well and love Jesus fully. It's a glimpse into the inner workings of the minds of teenagers and how I have been transformed, and what I have learned, by spending time and sharing space with my students.

Ultimately, I want this book to illustrate the practical side of evangelization in a most challenging, judgmental, and cut-throat environment: a high school full of hormonally volatile, cliquish, know-it-all teenagers searching for meaning and purpose. At its root, evangelization is sharing the Truth in a dynamic and engaging way, remembering that Truth is not merely a concept or an idea one can simply learn by diligently studying a textbook. The Truth is a person, three in fact, one of whom became flesh to dwell among us so that we might personally encounter and fall deeply in love with him. Evangelization is not about merely demonstrating concepts or memorizing facts to be regurgitated on an exam. It is meant to be an exercise in building relationships, both with those whom we encounter and he who is the subject of those encounters and our evangelization. It is the process of witnessing to a Truth greater than all the things this world has to offer. Evangelization is the greatest adventure one can set out on, a chance to share and be changed by the realest, most beautiful thing in the universe: Truth.

Having learned what evangelization is and how to do it in a practical way with teenagers, I've begun to think of myself less as a teacher and more as a "classroom evangelist." Teachers pass out exams and assign lengthy homework, grading papers until the red pen is dry and eyes are crossed. But being a classroom evangelist allows me to introduce the Way, the Truth, and the Life to every person that steps into Room 24 with a passion and vigor that can transform the world. Change the word "classroom" to whatever you like: business-office evangelist, grocery-store-aisle evangelist, or complete-stranger-in-an-elevator evangelist. Those of us with the opportunity to witness to our faith, in every setting and at any moment, must remember that at the heart of evangelization is Jesus Christ, true God and true Man, who wants to meet us, love us, and transform us. This book is a snapshot of how that "meeting Jesus" has played out in a classroom full of fourteen-year-olds and how the principles learned there are applicable anywhere.

I hope you find yourself seated in a desk in Room 24, paper and pen ready to take notes, when all of a sudden student A says the most absurd thing you've heard all day, and you can't help but giggle. As you're seated in that desk, I hope you begin to reflect on the wisdom of student B as she ridiculously compares Beyonce's music to the choirs of angels singing hallelujah in heaven. I hope you welcome and relish her comparison of beauty and goodness with the pop culture in which she dwells. I hope you come to recognize the immense value of a good education with caring and thoughtful teachers and see the significant impact Catholic schools especially have had on our country and world. Most of all, as you settle into your desk in Room 24, I hope you begin to meet Jesus, not just in the crucifix hanging on the wall or in the lecture material being presented, but also in the students who fill the room with their energy, insight, joy, and curiosity. I hope you are inspired to step out and become an evangelist yourself, applying the lessons from this classroom to your daily life as you encounter those who need to meet Jesus. Welcome to Room 24.

CHAPTER 1

WHAT CAN'T YOU LIVE WITHOUT?

Student A: Miss Prejean, I like your Chacos. You look like you're ready to go on an adventure.

Me: Studying and teaching theology means I'm on an eternal adventure!

Student B: Way to make it weird, Miss P . . . .

A SIMPLE QUESTION

In the fall of 2008, I had the incredible opportunity to study abroad with the University of Dallas (UD) Sophomore Rome Program. At nineteen years old, I boarded a plane and headed off for what would be the greatest adventure of my life. I was of course excited—*who wouldn't be*? I had the whole of Europe as my playground and a thirst to see the world. But I was also anxious, because I knew that by the end of the semester I would have to choose my major and decide on an academic advisor. The excitement of Rome lay ahead of me, but so did the frightening realization that my future would be at least partially determined by the major I had to choose in just a few short months.

The semester flew by, each day more incredible than the last. I hiked Mount Vesuvius in Pompeii, stood in Corinth, Greece, and read Paul's letter to the early Christian community there, drank beer in Germany, hiked the Cliffs of Moher in Ireland, ate strudel in Austria, ran a foot race in Olympia, was hungry in Hungary (really—I ate only one meal over a three day visit there), and prayed in the most beautiful church in all of Christendom, St. Peter's Basilica, countless times. Traveling to more than a dozen countries was just one small part of the semester, though. We were there to learn, not just from the world we were discovering, but also from our remarkably intelligent professors. We read *The Merchant of Venice* and then went and stood on the Rialto with Dr. Gregory Roper. Ancient Greco-Roman art and architecture became our specialty, and Dr. Laura Flusche would point out the column style and estimated date of every building we passed. The history and philosophy of Western civilization was brought to life by Drs. Peter Hatlie and Brad Blue who taught us the texts of Plato, Euripides, and countless others, and then brought us to Greece to see the very land in which the ancient philosophers and historians lived and about which they wrote.

One course stood out above all the rest: Western Theological Traditions. It traced the development of theological thought from the earliest days of the Church to the Second Vatican Council in the 1960s. We were reading the first texts outlining the doctrines of Catholicism and then visiting the catacombs where the first Christians worshipped and were eventually buried. We studied Aquinas's *Summa* and then stood in the orange grove he walked through, where he could be found arguing aloud with himself to clarify his points. We discussed the rich depth of the Vatican II documents, learning that we hadn't even begun to feel the earthquake from the modern council that was meant to be St. John XXIII's "breath of fresh air" for the Church. While all the classes were enlightening and impactful, this one was slowly convincing me that maybe I wanted to major in theology.

Not only was the course fantastic, but the professor leading us through the material was simply stellar. Dr. Mark Lowery was what I had always pictured a college professor would be like. He wore plaid shirts and khaki pants with a pleat down the middle and he'd had a salt and pepper goatee longer than I'd been alive. Above all else, Dr. Lowery had a deep and abiding passion for theology, and he never missed an opportunity to teach us the Truths of the Faith. He would eat dinner with us in the cafeteria, sitting with a new group of students every evening. He would wander into the commons area the night before a big exam and offer to further explain concepts we were struggling with, sometimes lighting up his pipe and joining the smokers outside for some friendly theological banter. He was a regular at daily Mass in the tiny, fifteen-person chapel on campus, often leaving his copy of *Magnificat* on the chair closest to the door. We all knew that was his spot. Dr. Lowery's smile was contagious, his laughter booming, his mind brilliant, and his fatherly spirit a comfort to us all.

A couple of weeks before the semester ended, right before finals were scheduled to begin, Dr. Lowery offered to take a group of students into the city for a walk through Piazza Navona to see Bernini's Fountain of the Four Rivers and visit the Church of St. Agnes of Rome. We had learned about the piazza, but hadn't officially visited it in any of our classes, so I jumped at the chance to see more of the city I'd soon be leaving. About a dozen of us set off with Dr. Lowery, ready for one final full day in the Eternal City. After a few hours wandering through the piazza and praying at the remains of St. Agnes, the majority of the group disbanded, some heading off to find gelato or to the other side of the city to watch an evening sunset in St. Peter's Square. I found myself alone with Dr. Lowery, standing on the far end of the piazza, looking out at the vendors selling their wares and the tourists studying their guidebooks. With a mischievous smile, Dr. Lowery asked me if I wanted to see one last thing before heading back to campus. He promised me it would be worth the short walk, so I immediately said yes and we took off toward the Basilica of St. Augustine, home to a lesser-known Caravaggio painting, *Madonna di Loreto*, and the tomb of St. Monica, the diligently praying mother of the young, party-animal Augustine.

As we weaved through the throngs of people crowding the small cobblestone streets, Dr. Lowery and I began talking about the semester. I told him how much I had enjoyed each class and every trip I'd had the chance to take, and he shared with me how truly invigorating it had been to teach in the city that was home to the theological discipline, his first and truest love. As we reached the Basilica of St. Augustine, both winded from the brisk walk, we took a moment to sit down on the steps and catch our breath. There was a comfortable silence between us as we looked up at the façade of the church, and Dr. Lowery casually asked me if I had chosen a major yet. He had no idea that for the past week I'd been battling with myself, flip-flopping between two different options. The inquiry threw me a bit off guard, so I decided to answer his question with a question.

> *Me*: I'm having a hard time choosing between English and theology. What do you think I should major in?

> *Dr. Lowery*: Katie, let me ask you this: if you had to give
> up reading or studying one of those subjects . . . say,
> you can never read Shakespeare again, how would
> you feel? If you had to give up theology, what would
> you think of that? It comes down to a simple question,
> really. . . . What can't you live without?

When Dr. Lowery posed the question, "What can't you
live without?" on the steps of the basilica, I felt an instant
tug on my heart to focus on the study of God. The thought of
never studying God again was maddening. I couldn't walk
away from theology. . . it was the only subject I'd ever found
that had satisfied my appetite for Truth and also inspired me
to keep learning more. There would never be an end to the
discipline, because there is no end to God. An infinite subject
means there is an infinite amount to learn, an infinite amount
to discover, and an infinite amount with which to fall in love.
As explained by the Jesuit theologian Karl Rahner, to study
theology is to set sail in search of the infinite horizon. I would
be able to see the line splitting the water and the sky off in the
distance, but I would never reach that line. I would just go
further and further out to sea, the distance from the original
shore increasing as I dove further into the depths of God. As
my academic advisor at UD, Dr. Christopher Malloy would
later say, "we're going to go scuba diving into Truth!" To study
God would be to study the realest, most complete thing in
the universe. It would be an active approach to his presence,
day in and day out. I would never become bored because I
would never exhaust the endless wealth of information there
was to gain. Dr. Lowery posed a question on the steps of that
church that rocked my world, and I instantly realized that,
more than anything else, I would rather be studying and sharing theology.

PALPABLE PASSION

As a kid, I hated math. My brain just didn't work in a mathematical way. I struggled for years with the subject and spent many a night at the kitchen table reviewing problems with my mom and dad, one a very successful business-owning CPA and the other vice-president and security director of a bank. I was the child of number-crunching people who was tortured on the regular by algebra, geometry, and calculus. My parents didn't want me to just make decent grades in math—they wanted me to really enjoy the subject. They had always taught me that memorizing concepts wasn't enough when it came to school. Learning shouldn't be about memorization and regurgitation, nor should it be a torturous experience—it is supposed to be an exercise in understanding the Truth, and the Truth should be exciting and fulfilling, whether it comes by way of math, biology, English, or history. Despite their valiant efforts, the "let's help Katie love math" project of the early 2000s failed miserably. I hated math, math hated me, and there was no resolving our numerous issues. I could solve at least one problem correctly: Katie + math homework = disaster, tears, and wailing and gnashing of teeth. I was doomed to a life of struggling in the subject, and I accepted my fate.

Then I met and was taught by Ms. Lynn Ruozzi, who taught Algebra I at my high school. Ms. Ruozzi had a love of numbers that was felt the second you stepped foot in her classroom. She made the subject fun and math became a bit more tolerable in my ninth-grade year. The next year, a veritable legend in the halls of St. Louis Catholic High, Mrs. Debbie Herpin, taught me geometry. A healthy mix of stern and sweet, she was a stickler for the dress code and hated when students chewed gum, but she also loved formulas, theorems, and proofs. She even wrote raps and performed them to teach us how to solve for the area of various shapes. I then had Mrs. Linda Gail Shumaker, the only person who, up to that point, made "solving for x" less of a guessing game and more of a scavenger hunt for the right number hidden in the formula that needed to be used. She and math were best friends, and she made no secret of the fact that she loved teaching it. My last year of high school, Mr. Casey Vincent, my student council advisor and mentor, taught me pre-calculus, making himself available for tutoring every day I needed it so that I could get the grade I wanted. With chalk-covered pants and a slight twinkle in his eye, he never turned me away when I had a question or needed help. It never seemed to matter if I was having trouble with math or with life; he made time for me.

I was taught my least favorite subject by some of my favorite teachers, men and women who saw not just the material and a student struggling with it but the chance to influence a heart just as much as they helped mold a mind. I wasn't just a student whose name was slapped on the top of a test with half the problems solved incorrectly, a hopeless case with a brain far more equipped to read words than analyze numbers. I was a student for whom they wanted to make math meaningful, and they were willing to help me. They loved their subject, deeply, and wanted me to love it too, or at least endure it to the point of not being utterly miserable.

They had a palpable passion. You could feel it in their classrooms—a tangible, demonstrable excitement about their subject that they wanted to convey and share with their students. Even if a kid hated math, like I did, we couldn't help but love the teacher because we knew the teacher loved us. The subject was important, yes, but the student learning the subject was the priority, whether they were breezing through the class with all As or struggling to squeak out a D.

When I began teaching in August 2012, three of those four teachers were still teaching at my high school. I wanted to model my approach after theirs, showing a love for theology that students would be able to recognize and be inspired by from day one. On the steps of a church in Rome I had decided to focus on the study of God, and now here I was with a classroom of my own to share the knowledge I had gained. I wanted to convey the same excitement they and many other teachers had shown me. I wanted my subject to be as powerful to my students as it was to me, and I wanted to show them I cared as much about them as my math teachers had cared about me.

The first lecture I gave in my classroom the first week of school was, in my utterly biased opinion, nothing short of epic. Based on the opening chapters of Frank Sheed's *Theology and Sanity*, I explained to my students how my class, Theology I, was the study of reality, because God is the realest thing in the universe. To gain knowledge of him would be to meet the Creator face to face, helping them see the rest of the world and study every subject in the proper light of his existence. I explained to them that to not study God, or to not even believe in God, would be to ignore reality, making the non-studying, non-believing person insane. That's the definition of insanity—to ignore reality. I was as simple and straightforward as I thought I could be, and I was positive I knocked the opening lecture out of the park. I just knew that these freshmen were going to love theology more than I did by the end of the year. *I was convinced.*

But then, in the last class on the Friday of that first week, a student sitting in the front row raised his hand at the end of my rousing lecture. He politely asked me if I could prove God's existence to him. Here was my moment: I could show off all that technical, hard-hitting theology I'd so diligently studied in college, making that absurdly expensive framed piece of paper hanging in my house worth it. I turned to the board, blue Expo marker in hand, and began outlining Thomas Aquinas's Five Proofs of God's Existence, beginning with the Argument from Motion. Arrowed diagrams began filling up the board next to a "timeline of existence" I had quickly scribbled. From there, I launched into the Argument from Causality and was just about to begin explaining the Argument from Governance when the bell rang. Students (who had gotten far more than they bargained for in the first week of Theology I) quickly began packing up their backpacks, ready to rush out probably hoping to never see me again. But the student who had posed the question held back and approached me.

> *Student*: Miss Prejean, I appreciate you explaining all that, but I just don't think God is real. There's just no way.

What wisdom this kid had! He was exhibiting such powerful intelligence by claiming to not believe the sheer genius of St. Thomas Aquinas, one of the greatest minds this world has ever known. Of course this fourteen-year-old was correct, there most certainly wasn't a God because if a high school freshman boy couldn't grasp his existence, then there's no way it could be true. Obviously! Or not . . .

It had been a long first week. I was tired, my hand was a bit sore from the death grip I'd had on the marker, and now I had a teenager declaring himself an atheist at the ripe, old age of fourteen. I was done, spent, mentally exhausted, and physically drained, so what I said next was naïve, arrogant, and just plain stupid. It is perhaps the moment I regret most in the course of my teaching career, the first-week blunder I never would have made had I followed the examples of my favorite teachers who had taught me my least favorite subject years before in the very same school.

> *Me*: If you don't believe in God then you're just ignoring reality, and that's insane.

INVITATION TO BELIEVE

The weeks following my encounter with that particular student were quite challenging. The Tuesday after I called him insane, he came into class with a list of questions about God, Catholicism, evolution, and scripture. A week after I called him insane, he brought in a copy of *The God Delusion* by Richard Dawkins and proceeded to read it in the front row while I taught the class. A month after I called him insane, he turned in his first test thirty seconds after I passed it out, "The Bible is the greatest fairytale ever told" written in every blank. Six weeks into the year, he transferred to another school, his parents citing "unresolvable differences" with the vision of the school and "consistent disagreements" with a certain teacher in Room 24.

Within two months of beginning my teaching career, I had managed to drive a student out of the only Catholic high school in our diocese because I was mostly concerned about proving a point to convince him I was right and he was wrong. Not only had I done exactly what my favorite teachers would never have done but I also ignored the examples of Jesus and the saints throughout the history of the Church.

While standing before him for sentencing, Jesus Christ didn't answer Pontius Pilate's query, "What is Truth?" with a scoffing laugh, shaking his head and saying, "Wouldn't you like to know!" When St. Peter began preaching to the large crowds of people after the descent of the Holy Spirit on

Pentecost, I doubt he would have looked at anyone express-
ing disagreement and said, "Well, you're just insane." In a
debate on matters of doctrine, St. Augustine certainly didn't
turn to his opponent and declare his argument null and void
with the charge, "That's absurd, and you're wrong." If Mother
Teresa were to encounter a man or woman dying in a ditch
who had no belief in the one, true God, her reaction would
not be to turn them away but rather to welcome them, care
for them, and love them no differently than she would any
faithful Christian. But I am not Jesus, Sts. Peter or Augustine,
or Blessed Mother Teresa of Calcutta.

No, I am arrogant, have-to-be-right-all-the-time, consistent sinner Katie Prejean, who on a Friday in August of 2012
looked at a fourteen-year-old boy and told him he was insane
because he didn't believe in God. This is certainly not the evangelization tactic Jesus Christ envisioned his followers would
one day utilize. Jesus told his disciples to "Go therefore and
make disciples of all nations . . . teaching them to obey everything that I have commanded you" (Mt 28:19a, 20a). He did
not say "Cut them down at the knees and then they'll believe
us!" Jesus Christ did not insult the non-believer and criticize
the sinner. He ate dinner with them. He didn't look at people
questioning his teachings and call them insane. He explained
it to them on their terms by telling parables and performing
miracles. When someone pressed Jesus for a deeper explanation, he gave it, not because he just wanted to prove a point
but because he wanted to actively, personally illustrate the
Truth. Jesus Christ did not come just to teach us a list of things
to memorize and recite. He came to save us. He came to build
a relationship with us. He came to love us. If we are going to
follow his explicit command to "do as I have done for you,"
then our approach to evangelization must be modeled after
his. It is not our primary task to prove a point. Our first job is

to love those whom we have the chance to teach, and the point proving will follow in due time.

We must first become like Christ and meet people where they are, see them for who they are, and love them there. The "I'm right, you're wrong" mentality must be struck from the script when we evangelize. Better yet, we should burn the script and bury the ashes because a cookie-cutter approach to sharing the Truth is a surefire way to ensure someone will walk away from the experience with a bad taste in his or her mouth. There's no denying that Jesus never wavered in teaching the Truth, standing his ground as he built the Kingdom. But he stood that ground by being grounded in charity, filled with compassion for the people whose very lives he created and saved. Jesus knew that acceptance of the Truth is personal, not something to be forced. He did not shove the Gospel down people's throats, causing them to choke on his words. Jesus presented his message and then let people choose to accept it on their own. This "freedom to choose" is at the heart of Jesus's preaching, seen in both the story of the rich young man and the Bread of Life discourse.

When a wealthy young man approaches Jesus, curious about how he can gain eternal life, Jesus's answer to "keep the commandments" doesn't seem to satisfy him. This young man claims he already follows these commands, so he asks, "What do I still lack?" indicating that he wants to go beyond the bare minimum. The rich young man is clearly yearning for something deeper, hoping to discover that which will satisfy a desperate longing in his heart. He is experiencing the deep internal dissatisfaction that St. Augustine wrote about centuries later: "Our hearts are restless until they rest in You, O Lord." Jesus sees into the young man's heart, recognizes his desire, and extends an invitation that will surely help him grow: "If you wish to be perfect, go, sell your possessions and give the money to the poor, and you will have treasure in heaven; then come, follow me." Jesus knew what held the young man back from the Truth and invited him to let go of the attachments that weighed him down so that the young man could gain what he desperately wanted. The Truth is laid out before the rich young man. Here are the instructions that must be followed to satisfy his deepest desire to gain eternal life and live the abundant life the Lord promises. Jesus could be no more clear and concise! But the rich young man can't accept it. He can't fathom a world in which his possessions are not primary, and so he walks away sad (see Mt 18:16–22).

Rather than point and laugh at the young man who has been sobered by his deep attachment to stuff, Jesus turns to his apostles and assures them that anyone, even the most materialistic of people, can be saved through the power of God. Jesus doesn't run after the young man and grab him by the collar, fussing at him for being so stupid and arrogant and insisting he listen to what he has to say. Jesus simply continues to explain to his disciples that this life of denial and sacrifice for God will pay dividends countless times over in the next life. Jesus lets the young man walk away and focuses his attention on those still present with him, imploring them to remain faithful to what he has said and assuring them of salvation if they do so.

We see a similar approach to ministry in the sixth chapter of John's gospel. After Jesus boldly proclaims his flesh is true food and his blood true drink, many people in the crowd "turned back and no longer went about with him." Jesus doesn't run after them, wagging his finger in their faces and fussing at them for denying what he just taught. He doesn't raise his voice and insist they continue listening to him lest they burn in hell for eternity. He doesn't pull the "God card" and assert great power. No, Jesus does none of that. Instead, his calm, peaceful response is one from which we must learn. Again, we see Jesus turn to his disciples and ask them, "Do you also wish to go away?" He poses a question that invites his followers to acknowledge whether or not they have embraced the Truth. Simon Peter's response is simple and beautiful, showing that he and the rest of the apostles have accepted the Truth personally and allowed it to take root in their hearts: "Lord, to whom can we go? You have the words of eternal life. We have come to believe and are convinced that you are the Holy One of God" (Jn 6:66–69). Jesus does not look at anyone and call him or her insane for rejecting what he has said. Instead, he turns to the apostles who are already accepting the Truth and invites them to launch further in. Perhaps the greatest way to love both the rich young man and the crowd of doubting listeners was to let them go off and ponder what he had said and allow them to accept the Truth at a time when they were ready to receive it.

Jesus was certainly right in what he preached to the rich young man and to the multitudes of listeners. We can't be attached to the things of this world if we want to love God fully, nor can we deny the validity of his flesh and blood as our one true source of eternal nourishment and salvation. God did not create humanity to be mindless robots forced to follow him, but instead he created us in his image and likeness with free will and the ability to choose. Likewise, Jesus lets those whom he heals and to whom he preaches freely choose whether to believe the Truth or to reject it. The invitation Jesus extends is not a mandate for belief or a command to worship. He does not force acceptance. We get to choose. Belief in the Truth is an opportunity laid before us, an invitation to a relationship that can be freely accepted or declined.

If we are forced to believe anything, the belief rings hollow. If we are forced to do anything, the action is less meaningful.

When my mom made me clean my room as a kid, she would always follow her demand with, "I want you to want to clean your room." My violin instructor ended each lesson with the reminder that "you should choose to practice thirty minutes every day to become the best you can be." The first question a couple is asked in their marriage vows is, "Have you come here freely and with full consent?" We are a people designed for choice, created by a God who chose to give us life and then freely chose to die for us. When we freely choose to accept the invitation to his Truth, our belief will ring out with the melody of love.

Those of us who have accepted the invitation and have chosen the Truth have an obligation to share what we know to be beautiful, fulfilling, and good. But herein lies a lofty challenge: extending an invitation to the Truth rather than forcing a point. We may have sold our possessions and walked away from the world to follow Christ, at least in some way, but the majority of people to whom we are called to share the Truth with have not even come close to doing that. We may believe in the Eucharist as the source and summit of our faith, but those to whom we are called to speak may think we're crazy for consuming what still looks like bread and wine and calling it Christ. We may have five very detailed proofs for God's existence and believe he is real, but the fourteen-year-old student who tells you he thinks God isn't real doesn't care about Aquinas's arguments in the least. The goal is not to prove our point. The goal is to extend an invitation to believe. This is a critical first step in evangelization: to open our arms and invite others to approach the Truth we so dearly love, welcoming them and giving them a real chance to choose.

CHAPTER 2

WHERE JESUS IS LORD

Student A: Hey, Miss Prejean, why do you have that sign outside your door, the one that says, "Where Jesus Is Lord"?

Me: Oh, it's an inside joke with a student who graduated a couple years ago; I should probably just take it down.

Student B: Well if you take it down, don't you think you'll offend Jesus? He is the Lord in here.

Student A: Yeah, you can't kick Jesus out! That's like a free ride to hell in a Ferrari, Ms. P.!

Student B: Riding in a Ferrari would be cool though . . . take it down. Definitely. Jesus will just have to deal.

A NEW PRIORITY

The January of my first year of teaching, I was given the daunting task of planning the senior retreat, an overnight, out-of-town, "Kumbaya" session meant to bond the class together. I had always thought the senior retreat was a bit pointless: Let's make these kids fall in love with the school and each other five months before we watch them graduate and run as far away from high school as possible. I'm nothing if not obedient, though, so I willingly accepted the task with a smile and set out to plan the most epic spiritual experience these seniors could ever have, all on a shoestring budget and with less than ten days' prep time. A veteran of retreat planning and staffing, I was resolved to succeed in creating a stellar retreat, regardless of the challenges placed before me. I wanted the students to not only recognize the value of one another, something essential to the retreat's focus, but also realize the importance of an authentic relationship with Jesus. I didn't want them to just sing campfire songs and hold hands—I wanted them to have the chance to genuinely reflect on their faith journey and make conscious efforts and practical changes to improve their spirituality.

God answered my prayers in spades that weekend. Over the course of thirty-six hours, the students were able to tear down walls and build bridges within their class, as well as search within themselves for deeper meaning and focus in their spiritual journey. In the first few hours of the retreat, we had students write one word that described how they felt about themselves and their relationship with God at that point in their lives. We taped the papers to the wall, a collage of soul-searching on display for each student to see. The words were varied: scared, indistinguishable, restless, open, nervous, ready, content. The faces of the students as they stood there and stared at each paper captured countless emotions. It was as if each one was seeing themselves and their peers with newly opened eyes, recognizing that together they were anxious about the future and unsure of their next steps. These students had spent much of the previous three and a half years together, but they were only just now meeting each other for the first time.

There was a new day dawning on the senior class as they entered more fully into the retreat experience. It was obvious the Holy Spirit was working. They had the chance to share and forgive one another for past wrongs committed. They spent time in adoration of the Blessed Sacrament. They completed various ropes course challenges, which pushed them to their mental and physical limits. As the retreat was coming to a close and the group was making its way to the cafeteria for our last meal before heading back to town, one of the senior boys walked up to me and struck up a conversation.

> *Student*: Have you noticed what all the signs around here say, Miss Prejean?
>
> *Me*: Yeah, they all say "Where Jesus Is Lord" after the building description. It's kind of funny.
>
> *Student*: Cafeteria . . .
>
> *Me*: Where Jesus Is Lord.
>
> *Student*: Boys Dorm . . .
>
> *Me*: Where Jesus Is Lord!
>
> *Student*: Gun Range . . .
>
> *Me*: Where Jesus Is Lord!

He and I laughed as we continued along the gravel path toward the cafeteria. I didn't know this young man well. In fact, I found it a little odd that he had started walking with me in the first place. All weekend he'd seemed a little aloof and checked out of the retreat experience, and I had assumed he didn't really care about being there. We'd mutually ignored each other for the entire weekend, but here he was, joking with me about the ridiculous signs announcing every room (including the bathrooms) as a place "Where Jesus Is Lord!"

So, taking a shot in the dark, I decided to ask him what he thought about the retreat.

> *Student*: I think it was good. A lot of the guys were say-
> ing in the dorm last night that it wasn't as bad as they
> expected, so that means they liked it. And I liked it, too.
>
> *Me*: What was your favorite part?
>
> *Student*: Seeing those signs.

Confused by his answer, I pressed him for more information.

> *Me*: The signs? What about the signs made it your
> favorite part?
>
> *Student*: Well, Jesus is Lord, and I think a lot of us
> are going to start acting like that's true. He's Lord of
> everything around here and they put it on all these
> signs, which is a good reminder. You know, for the first
> time, I'm starting to notice he should be the Lord of my
> heart, too. So even if I don't really see or hang out with
> my classmates after we graduate, at least I got that out
> of all this, and that's my favorite thing about it.

I continued walking in stunned silence. I couldn't believe that this young man whom I hadn't exchanged ten words with prior to that moment had just captured the entire purpose of the retreat by pointing out signs I had thought were ridiculous and that I had secretly made fun of. I had hoped the retreat would introduce the seniors to Christ, at the very least. Yet here was a student telling me that he had not only heard about Jesus but had personally encountered him as Lord and wanted to make Jesus *the* priority in his life.

MEETING JESUS

All people, especially high school students, struggle to find out who they are and what to do with their lives. In the great search for identity, people have started to realize they don't know themselves in the slightest, especially who they are as children of God made in his image and likeness. We have forgotten both who we are and whose we are, so we seek definition in the fleeting things placed before us. Every day I watch my students conform to the newest trend and most popular fad trying to be acceptable to their peers. They want to both see and be seen. This conformity isn't limited to high school students of course. All people seek acceptance and meaning. All of us look for direction and purpose and hope to learn what we should do when we arrive. We are all on a quest to find something greater than what this often shallow, quickly passing world has to offer. We are looking for the Truth.

In the first chapter of John's gospel, there is a beautiful and poignant moment between Jesus and two of his would-be followers. As Jesus walks by, John the Baptist boldly announces him as the "Lamb of God," piquing the interest of Andrew and another unnamed man. They approach Jesus who asks them what they are seeking. Hoping to find out where Jesus is staying, they question him about his plans, and they are quite surprised with his answer. "Come and see," Jesus tells them, and so they go and spend the day with him. Rather than outlining his agenda for the next three years of his public ministry or giving them an address of the place where he would be spending the night, Jesus extends an invitation to these two men to come and be with him, thus changing their lives, and the lives of countless others, forever. Andrew and his companion encountered Jesus Christ that day. They saw him, spoke with him, and spent time and shared space with

him. They met the Lord, and as Andrew would later tell his
fisherman brother, Simon Peter, they found the Messiah. This
encounter with Christ profoundly changes Andrew and eventually Peter. They become active, faithful followers of this man
who was pointed out to them, who simply invited them to
"come and see."

It is a personal, unique encounter with Jesus, just like the
one Andrew had, that deeply transforms someone—that gives
him or her purpose and meaning for which we all strive. As we
meet Jesus face to face in the Eucharist, through the prayerful
reading of scripture, in the confessional receiving forgiveness,
or as we see him in the people surrounding us, we are more
fully and authentically formed in his image and likeness. We
begin to decrease and Christ begins to increase. This, then,
should be a top priority in evangelization: to create opportunities to meet Christ who will then transform the lives of those
who encounter him.

If my students memorize the Ten Commandments and
recite the Beatitudes then they will pass my tests and have
a great party trick for college. If they are not following those
Commandments and living out those Beatitudes then I have
failed them as a classroom evangelist. I have slowly learned
that it is not me my students need to know nor is it my technical content that they should remember for years to come. It
is Jesus Christ they must meet, it is Jesus they should learn,
and it is Jesus they will grow to love. This personal encounter
with Christ is at the heart of our existence and is the very root
of evangelization. Personally meeting Jesus is the foundation
upon which we know, love, and serve him. It is the center of
all any of us will ever do in service to him and his Church.
When we invite anyone to personally meet Jesus face to face,
to come and see him, we begin to see the person change into
a follower and then be transformed into a believer.

I have watched my freshmen struggle to find identity and purpose, and the best antidote to the problem is simply to teach Jesus. All too often, though, I have made the mistake of teaching *about* Jesus, harping on theological points rather than sharing a person. There is certainly a benefit to learning the intricacies of Christology, but that is not often the solution to helping someone discover the purpose he or she desperately seeks. To "teach Jesus" means we don't just list off his attributes, define his qualities, memorize his miracles, or discuss his Resurrection. To teach Jesus is to show the face of Christ by being his hands and feet to one another. It is to illustrate how the Son of Man lived out what he preached and to introduce those around us to the Word made Flesh dwelling among us and within us. To teach Jesus is to conform ourselves, and help to form others, into "little Christs" who go out and share the Good News. People are not easily transformed by ideas and concepts alone. They are far more often transformed by other people. If we want to help others discover their true identities, we must first introduce them to the very person who gives meaning to their existence—Christ Jesus.

Evangelization begins by recognizing that those to whom we witness have to make their own choices to believe and engage with Christ. We cannot force them to listen, we cannot demand they accept the Truth, and we cannot focus only on proving our arguments. We can invite, and once they've chosen to listen and are open to belief, then we have the awesome chance to introduce them to their creator, savior, and constant helper. When we evangelize, we stand at this threshold between invitation and acceptance and welcome them into personally meeting the Lover of Souls. We share with them a person, the God-man, who himself chose to step into our world for a specific purpose: to encounter us one-on-one and tell us he is the Way we should walk, the Truth we should believe, and the abundant Life into which we are joyfully welcomed.

When that student looked at me and said he had enjoyed the retreat, I knew what we did had "worked." The points we made and the concepts we taught had been thoroughly learned and believed. But when he said he was going to make Christ the Lord of his heart, I knew that he had met Jesus and been profoundly changed by the encounter. There was no better outcome to be achieved!

A week after the retreat, as I pulled open the door to the theology department foyer and flipped on the light, I noticed a piece of construction paper taped to the wall right outside my classroom door. In big bold letters, the sign read, "Miss Prejean's Room: Where Jesus Is Lord."

CHAPTER 3

SEVENTY-TWO PERCENT COMPATIBLE

Student A: Miss Prejean, other than him being Catholic and employed, what else do you look for in a future husband?

Me: Well, it would be nice if he was a good dancer, since I love to dance.

Student B: It's weird you'd want him to be good at something you're not good at . . . poor guy.

STRANGE FRIENDS

I was in eleventh grade when I created my Facebook profile, proud to be among the first five students at my high school to have one. These were the early days of Facebook, before *liking* everything and the never-truly-finished chat box conversations with the *seen at* notification. This was when photos had to be painfully uploaded from a computer and before glowing screens in our pockets could instantly update us on the whereabouts and goings-on of anyone we've ever met. To post a status you had to fill in the blank, a present-tense update structured according to Zuckerberg's rules. But as the Internet grew, and access to the World Wide Web became nearly instant and everywhere, so too did social media. With Facebook statuses came Twitter updates, 140-character statements used in battles of wit and relevance. Then Instagram joined in, the hub of filtered photos and endless hashtags. I took the Internet bait, hook, line, and sinker, becoming an overly active social media consumer and user.

The more followers I gained, the better. The more likes, retweets, and shares, the more validated and confident I felt. It was like a drug. Each moment I spent building up my online presence was more of a high than the last. With the rise of being noticed on the Internet, though, came the potential of being befriended and followed by unknown individuals from around the world. There was the occasional student that slipped through the cracks, causing me to go on a "block all the followers" purge, and from time to time a complete stranger would find me on Facebook and request to be my friend. I'd ignore the request, citing the fact that Facebook was more of a place for people I actually knew in real life.

In late March, 2014, while enjoying a rare night at home without tests to grade or lesson plans to complete, I was wasting time browsing Buzzfeed and scrolling through my Facebook newsfeed. The Facebook notification sound dinged on my computer as a friend request came through. A man named Patrick had added me as a friend. After looking at his profile, I realized I didn't recognize him and denied the friend request. I thought nothing of it. Facebook doesn't send a notification when a friend request is denied, so I didn't really think this Patrick fellow would even notice. As I made my way into the kitchen to fix dinner, the notification sound dinged again. I quickly looked at the screen and saw that Patrick had added me as a friend again; keeping with my previous action, I denied the request. As I came back into the living room, dinner in hand, I saw that he had added me as a friend a third time.

I racked my brain trying to remember if I knew this guy from anywhere, because he clearly wanted to be my friend on Facebook. I didn't recognize his face, I had never heard the name, and we were four years apart in age so I knew we hadn't gone to high school together. For the third time that night, I denied Patrick's friend request. A window instantly popped up on my screen, and the Facebook security robot courteously asked me if I knew him in real life. I selected the option "I do not know this person" and closed my laptop, not giving the three-time friend request of Patrick another thought. I went about my evening, enjoying the lack of work I had. I watched a few episodes of some mindless show on Netflix before climbing in bed with the intent of reading myself to sleep. As I began to doze off, ready to turn out the light and catch up on some much-needed sleep, my phone rang.

It is a rare thing for my phone to ring. Most people that have my number know that e-mails or texts are the best way to find me, and probably the quickest way for me to reply. But there it was, my phone vibrating on the nightstand as I was beginning to fall asleep at 10:30 at night. The number was unknown and it was late, so my impulse was to let the call go straight to voicemail. But knowing I had youth group teens about forty-five minutes away setting up for a diocesan youth conference at a retreat center with limited cell service, I was worried something had gone wrong and they might be trying to get in touch with me.

"Hello?" I said as I answered the call. My greeting was met with silence. "Hello? This is Katie." Still no response. "Is anyone there? Hello?" Just as I was about to hang up the phone, someone spoke.

"Good evening, Miss Prejean. How are you?"

I thought maybe a student had somehow found my phone number and was calling to ask me about a homework assignment or upcoming test.

"Who is this? How did you find this number?" I sternly asked, ready to figure out which student was going to get a harsh talking to about respecting boundaries, privacy, and our diocesan safe environment policy the next morning.

"This is Patrick, Miss Prejean. How are you this evening?"

Immediately recognizing the name, I quickly asked, "How did you find this number, Patrick?"

Clearly flustered, he began breathing heavily into the phone. "I . . . ummmm . . . how are you? How has your day been?"

Ready to hang up the phone, I asked one last time, "How did you get this number, Patrick?" More silence.

"I don't know you and I would appreciate if you didn't use this number again," I said. Just as I was about to end the call, he began explaining himself, talking at lightning speed.

"I saw your profile on Christian Mingle earlier tonight and I googled your name and I found your phone number on your website and blog and I just was hoping maybe we could . . . I just think we have a lot in common . . . so I was kind of hoping we could maybe grab . . . "

I stopped him mid-sentence. "Patrick, please don't call this number again. I'm not really interested in dating anyone right now, especially someone I've never met who found me on the Internet. Have a good night." I hung up the phone and sat on the edge of my bed, confused.

I didn't have a Christian Mingle profile, and I was pretty sure my phone number wasn't on my website for my speaking ministry, but that's how he said he'd found me. Flustered and a bit concerned, I turned out the light and tried to fall asleep, to no avail. Patrick kept calling back, five times in the three minutes before I blocked the number, called my dad, and told him what happened. As soon as he stopped laughing about the absurdity of me having an Internet-dating stalker, he came over to make sure my alarm system was in proper working order before I went back to bed and attempted to fall asleep.

When I woke up the next morning and began to get ready for the day, the events of the previous evening kept running through my mind. A complete stranger had found a Christian Mingle profile on me that I knew nothing about and then added me as a friend on Facebook three times in the span of fifteen minutes, and after being denied each time, he had tracked down my phone number and called me up at 10:30 at night to ask me out on a date. The whole situation was just bizarre.

School was far too busy for me to think about it all throughout the day, though. I was giving a quiz to every class, followed by a lecture on how each of the twelve apostles died. Thoughts of Patrick and the strange phone call were trumped by recounting the upside down crucifixion of St. Peter and the flaying of St. Bartholomew. After finishing the lecture early in my third period class, the students and I began to chat about nothing and everything. I had finally seen a movie they'd all insisted I watch, and we were commiserating about how the book is always better than the film version. Students were begging me for insider info about whether or not the rumors were true about me teaching junior theology the next year, and then we started laughing about a caricature of me at my future wedding that a student had recently drawn on the back of her test.

Amidst the banter, I suddenly remembered everything from the night before and decided to fill them in on yet another awkward pseudo-romantic encounter in my young life.

> *Me*: The strangest thing happened last night, y'all. This guy kept adding me as a friend on Facebook, and then he tracked down my phone number and called me to ask me out. It was the weirdest thing.
>
> *Student*: What was the guy's name, Miss Prejean?
>
> *Me*: Oh, that's not important . . . it's just something weird that happened. I thought y'all might find it funny. He said he found me on Christian Mingle, which I assure y'all, I do NOT have a profile on that website.
>
> *Student*: Was his name Patrick, Miss Prejean?
>
> *Me*: Ummm . . . how did you know that?
>
> *Student*: Well. You see . . . I kind of . . . I thought it would be a good idea if we . . . I created a . . .
>
> *Me*: You created a Christian Mingle account for me!? You did not do that! What have you done?!
>
> *Student*: I just didn't want you to be lonely anymore, Miss Prejean. I know you want to have kids someday and we all would really love to see you happy, and I figured if I helped you find a husband, then maybe you'd invite me to your wedding someday . . .
>
> *Me*: I am not going to meet my future husband on the Internet or Christian Mingle, not to mention the fact that this is an extreme violation of privacy and is completely inappropriate!! You need to delete that account right now! Right. Now!
>
> *Student*: I'll delete it, I promise. But will you at least look at Patrick's page? He sent a wink to your profile yesterday.

> *Me*: He sent a what?! This guy found my private information online and then called me multiple times last night after I told him I wasn't interested. I am not looking at his profile, and I am not going out with him. You need to delete that account you made for me right now!
>
> *Student*: But Miss Prejean, Christian Mingle said y'all were seventy-two percent compatible . . .

INVESTMENT RETURNS

After the dust settled from the realization that one of my fourteen-year-old students had gone on the Internet and created a dating profile for me, I noticed there was something heartfelt in what he had said: "We all would really love to see you happy." Over the course of the previous seven months of the school year, my students had grown to see me as more than just a talking head standing in front of a white board wielding an Expo marker. I was a real person to them. I was someone with feelings and opinions, someone who knew the plot twists of teen drama shows like *Gossip Girl* and wanted to get married and have children someday. I had deep desires and maddening fears that I wasn't afraid to share with my students. I had told them that I, too, struggled to follow God's will and that I wrestled daily with self-doubt and worry. I was a person just like them, only a decade older with a few more mistakes to my name. I was making my way through this confusing, tumultuous, joy-filled life the same way they were, and showing them that made me a real person with a real life who could evangelize and teach in a relatable, personal, effective way. It's why they were able to ask:

> *Student A*: Miss Prejean, if you get married while we're still students here, can we come to your wedding in our uniforms?

Me: Ummm . . . no. That's weird.

Student B: Okay, what about your funeral? Can we come to that in our uniforms?

I began doing something very simple at the beginning of my second year of teaching. I stand at the door to my classroom and hand each wide-eyed, unsuspecting freshman an index card. They're given specific instructions: write your name, birthday, and a joke on the card and be prepared to share a fun fact about yourself with the class. The next seventy minutes are then spent getting to know one another. The activity is simple, almost stupid, but it accomplishes a specific purpose: the ice is broken and the fears of having a huge load of homework on the first night of school are relieved. It also helps me learn names much quicker than if I just study a roster with each student's picture because now I have some goofy factoid to associate with each one. To this day, the young lady who told me that she really liked a certain food is still called by the nickname she earned that day: Pickles.

I wanted to convince my students that mine would be a classroom where each and every one of them could be completely themselves. Bring it all in: the weird goofiness, the obsession with Taylor Swift, the fear of being judged coupled with the fear of not being noticed, the doubt about God's existence, the confusion about life's purpose. Be you, and I will teach you and love you as you are. That was, and is, rule number one in Room 24. I wanted them to know that every godly desire would be pursued and every crippling fear would be swiftly dispatched. As their teacher, I would celebrate their successes and help them improve upon their failures. I wanted them to know that Room 24 would be a place where I would strive to see each one for who they were right then and there and help each one become the person God had made them to be. Each student was a beautiful, unique child of God and I had the chance to get to know each one, teach each one the Truth, and invest myself in each student's formation.

The investments I had made were beginning to pay dividends far quicker than I expected. In showing my own imperfections and struggles and in sharing pieces of my life with them, especially my personal faith, I had become someone my students cared about. My students' frequent questions of "How's your day been?" and "What'd you do last night?" or "What's your favorite prayer?" weren't simply silence fillers. My students were showing genuine interest in my life the same way I had shown genuine interest in theirs. I made an investment in them, and they in turn made an investment in me. I came to find out that most of the students in that third period class knew about the Christian Mingle profile. They also all knew about the Pinterest board students were contributing to for the future wedding they all hoped they would get invited to once they found me a husband. But they also all knew they could come to me for any reason to talk about anything. To them, I wasn't just "Miss Prejean in room 24" giving notes during the required class period and grading their homework. I wanted to be available to them, ready to provide the guidance and support they needed in whatever way I could, and I was.

Some students would come to Room 24 in tears, hurt by a friend and seeking comfort. Others would come angry about the injustice of a situation and want an adult perspective on the frequent unfairness of life. A few came with questions about faith, desperately hoping to understand what they wanted to believe. And some didn't ever come any time other than when they were told they had to set foot in my classroom for seventy minutes three times a week. But during the course of those class periods and lunchtime chats and random visits, I was there for them, seeing in each of them the beautiful mess that made every single one unique and showing them the same mess in my life, which then opened the door to more effectively teach faith and share Jesus. Because I was there for them, in so many different ways, they somehow thought if they made a dating profile and found me a husband, then they would be there for me, too.

PEOPLE, NOT PAPER

> *Student*: What kind of food are you gonna have at your wedding, Miss Prejean?
>
> *Me*: I have no idea. I'm not planning it yet . . .
>
> *Student*: Well, I have a Pinterest board for you. I think we should go with pancakes.

The opportunity to evangelize should never be used as an opportunity to merely pontificate, lecture, or deliver discourse. It is a chance to share your very self, making the stuff of faith come alive not with words alone but with showing and sharing your life. We must avoid becoming talking theological heads in the mission fields of classrooms, offices, grocery stores, or living rooms. Instead, we must share and be our truest selves: people transformed by the very love of the Person we teach.

Day to day and in various places, we have the chance to evangelize. We constantly encounter people who are messy, sinful, virtuous, beautiful, and far from perfect. The message we share and the Truth we teach and live cannot just be the stuff printed on paper and bound in thick textbooks. We must make an investment in every person we are blessed to encounter and evangelize, focusing not just on the concepts to be taught but concentrating most of our efforts on seeing them for who they are and showing them the Christ who has known them all along. People have to be met where they are, loved where they are, and taught where they are, and we must show them our most authentic selves—unique and messy in our own ways—as we meet, love, and teach them.

In order for evangelization to be effective we must build relationships with the people we evangelize. The same way we want to show the necessity and beauty of a personal relationship with Jesus, so too must we establish and foster relationships with the people we lead to Christ. We don't want people to just remember precepts and recite doctrine. That's just memorization, not learning nor living the Truth. So why do we so often evangelize in rote, repetitive, impersonal ways? Spouting out facts is not enough anymore, nor has it ever really been enough in the work of evangelization. We must focus on sharing the Truth with the people we encounter and stop clinging to the paper upon which is written the Truth we love. We have to do as Jesus himself did: engage the crowds, eat supper with the sinners, comfort the sorrowful, and wash the feet.

Jesus didn't wag his finger and fuss at the babies for screeching in the back pew during a too-long homily. He let the little children use him as a human (and divine) jungle gym. Jesus didn't tell the crowds to fend for themselves when they got restless and hungry. He increased what little was available and satisfied them abundantly. Jesus didn't make dinner reservations with the wealthy, fancy, most opportunistic folks in the town. He sat down with prostitutes and tax collectors, beggars and thieves, and told them they were as valuable and precious as the rich man denying them scraps from his table. Jesus looked into the eyes of the woman who touched his cloak and told her that her abundant faith had healed the hemorrhage that plagued her for twelve long years. He saw her for who she was, a broken, pained, tired woman, and he loved her in that brokenness and healed her in that exhaustive pain. Jesus got down on his hands and knees, taking on a task of servants and slaves as he washed off the dirt that was caked upon the feet of his closest friends and chosen followers. He humbled himself at dinner and showed his fear just a few hours later as he sweat blood and cried in the garden.

Is this not one of the many reasons the Jewish authorities hated him? They were scared of these unknown methods of preaching salvation. He was not standing in the temple reciting and diligently following the Law of Moses—what the Sanhedrin considered to be the holiest of tasks and the only worthy and dignified worship. In fact, Jesus was out breaking some of those laws, healing on the Sabbath and talking with Samaritan women next to wells. Jesus was a religious rebel, setting a model from which we could and rightly should learn.

Jesus did not hand out textbooks or issue exams. He did not print flyers and belabor the choosing of cheesy clipart for the weekly bulletin. Jesus did not insult, judge, isolate, or even retaliate (although we do have that one flipping tables incident, which means that flipping desks is always a valid course of action should a student become a bit too annoying). Jesus himself, the very man we teach and love, concentrated his efforts on meeting and loving people. He grew to know them, and they in turn grew to know him, the very Word made Flesh.

Jesus did not ask to read a résumé of the apostles. He called them by name, claimed them as his own, and then spent three years with them, sharing meals and letting them hear and see everything about him, even that which they didn't yet understand. Jesus got down in the dirt with Mary the prostitute and told her he didn't condemn her, and she became a steadfast follower, even finding the tomb empty three days after she stood at the foot of the cross and watched him die.

This is not to say procedures or methods or good textbooks should be burned and cast off; far from it. Classroom management is a must, sound theology is a given, and there should be a structure to what we do when we evangelize. If you walk up to a complete stranger in the food court at the local mall and begin to share your testimony of faith, it might not do much in the way of building the Kingdom. But when we are given the opportunity to encounter people, whether lifelong friends or friends waiting to be made, we must remember the structure and method we employ should be in service to the relationship we work to first establish, not the other way around.

Don't be the talking head with an idea to pontificate. Be a real person with a story and a passion for the Truth. Share yours, learn theirs, and introduce Jesus. Then watch the greatest of relationships begin to unfold. Who knows, maybe you'll find that you and the person you encounter and share faith with are seventy-two percent compatible!

CHAPTER 4

JOY DOWN IN THE HEART

Me: How do you make a hot dog stand?
Students: [Blank expressions]
Me: Take away its chair!
Student A: Do you have any idea how lame you are, Miss Prejean?
Student B: Lamer than the guys that Jesus healed in the gospels!

A BROKEN FUNNY BONE

I was never the funny one in my family. That honor went to my little sister, who taught herself to juggle when she was eight years old and carried joke books around so she could memorize new material for mealtime conversations. Laura would do stand-up routines after Sunday dinner at our great-aunt Mimi's house and organize karaoke sessions on holidays at Grandma's. After she lost her two front teeth within a few weeks of each other, Uncle Benny nicknamed her "Snaggle-tooth," adding to her comedic brilliance. In her high school years, Laura mastered the subtle art of sarcasm, making her darn near unstoppable. There was rarely a dull moment in conversation with Laura, and she always seemed to be enjoying herself, a happy-go-lucky kid with a carefree attitude. She was never bored, she wasn't stressed, and everyone thought she was just the cutest thing they ever did see when she flashed her dimpled smile.

Laura inherited the funny bone and we all knew it, and despite my human desire to be funny too, I accepted the fact that maybe the humor gene had somehow skipped me. While my sister was naturally clever with this streak of laughter-making running right through her, I was far more serious and straight-laced as a child. I wanted every moment of every day planned and organized. I knew where I was going, who was going to be there, what I was going to do, and I most certainly needed to be on time, if not early. I got my first watch for Christmas when I was just six years old, and I asked for a new one for my birthday just seven months later because I didn't want the cartoon Snow White and her seven stupid dwarves hanging out on my wrist.

My no-nonsense attitude followed me to high school and was probably the reason I only had a few close friends. They, of course, knew I wasn't the type of kid who would be absurdly silly for no good reason. I joined the clubs guaranteed to beef up my résumé, competing in speech and debate and running for student council. I followed the dress code to a T, insisting my mother lower the hem on my skirts so that there was no danger of getting a detention. At Friday night football games, I didn't sit in the student section: I was either in the stands with my parents or on the sidelines taking pictures for yearbook. And I sure as heck wasn't telling jokes or earning a reputation as a funny kid. In my mind, seriousness showed diligence and was the path to success. That guy working the counter at the fast food restaurant probably goofed off in high school, and I wanted to ensure I never fell into that trap.

Shortly after graduating, a friend of mine let it slip that my nickname for the past four years had been "stick-in-the-mud-Katie." I wouldn't say I was a stick-in-the-mud but rather a very focused, determined, diligent kid who wanted . . . Oh, who was I kidding? More suitable words about me had never been spoken!

I changed when I went off to college. What better time to reinvent myself than a new place six hours away from my hometown with people I'd never met before? There was no better place to become more relaxed, upbeat, and happy. I was studying and living in a place where frivolity and playfulness and laughter were inescapable, just as much in the classroom as out. For the first time in my life, I allowed myself to have fun, playing and singing Irish tunes in the woods with friends late into the night and laughing for hours between classes while sitting out on the patio at the cappuccino bar. There was a dynamic energy and tangible joy radiating across campus. It was as if someone had given me permission to let loose a bit and simply enjoy life, and the majority of people at UD, both students and professors, were of the same attitude.

Dr. Brownsberger let us crack open beers on the last day of his Christology course to celebrate four years of hard work earning our degrees, and after he was finished lecturing, he enjoyed one with us on a bench outside. Dr. Hanssen staged a break out every year from the Charity Week jail where students and professors could lock each other up for a dollar an hour to raise money for local organizations. Dr. Jodziewicz always played Santa at the student-government sponsored Christmas party. Fr. Maguire, the resident Cistercian monk who could always be found in his office willing to hear confessions or give a blessing, would bring Bailey's Irish crème to class on the last day of his Irish Literature course. Dr. Lowery, the same professor who had challenged me to focus my studies in theology, would begin each class with a groan-worthy joke often so cheesy it was good.

No student ever doubted the serious scholarship of the professors on campus. We knew we were beyond lucky to be taught by some of the finest minds in academia. But we also knew we were remarkably blessed to be in the company of people who enjoyed what they did and shared that joy with their students. It became obvious that school didn't have to be straight-laced and serious all the time. It could be, and frequently was, joyful and fun while also being productive. But I somehow forgot that joyful atmosphere I loved and embraced so deeply when I became a teacher myself.

HIDE THE SMILE

A few minutes before classes began on the first day of school my first year teaching, I found myself standing in the teacher break room, mindlessly stirring sugar into my freshly poured cup of coffee. I was nervous and excited all at the same time, unsure of how the first day would unfold. Teachers were milling around the room, some checking their mailboxes for lunch duty schedules and others commiserating about how classes were getting bigger and bigger each year. One of my coworkers saw me standing there gazing off into space and asked me if I was feeling alright. I told him I was a bit scared about what the kids would think of me, especially since I was so young, and I was nervous about how to interact with them in a professional, yet inviting, manner. I thought my concerns were valid, especially since I had no formal teacher training. My coworker patted me on the back and said, "Don't worry about that. Just tell them what I always say on the first day: 'I'm friendly, but I'm not your friend.' That'll get them to sit down and shut up real quick." He walked off with a smile, pleased with his clever line. Another teacher across the room chimed in. "I was told on my first day of teaching to never smile until midterms, that way they know you mean business. It's worked for me all these years," she said. A third teacher piped up with, "I abide by the rule that if the kids think you're having too much fun, they will probably start misbehaving. Just be serious and they'll know you mean business."

Seriousness, huh? That should be easy for me, I thought, especially since I'd spent my high school years as a student being just that in the very same school in which I now taught. I walked into my classroom, introduced myself to my students, and launched into explaining my rules with the words of my coworkers bouncing around in my mind. Be friendly, but don't befriend them. Hide your smile. This classroom is a business and you are the CEO, and CEOs surely don't laugh or smile. Be serious, Katie. Just be serious.

And I was. Students would come in, they would sit down, I would give notes, they would complete assignments and take tests, I would pass out grades, and we'd rinse and repeat it all the next day. Order would lead to success, surely. This was classroom management at its finest. With proper procedures and systematic efficiency, no one could accuse me of being a bad teacher. But I was doing a hack job of evangelization and relationship building. I was not truly teaching anything except organizational skills and how to complete a worksheet. At risk of becoming a slave to seriousness rather than an arbiter of

God's joy, I was making theology a miserable subject with no fun, frivolity, laughter, or excitement. I was miserable myself. Three months into school, my classroom was becoming a prison: Cell Block 24, a place I dreaded walking into just as much I imagined my students did. The humdrum drone of my lecturing voice was not making theology come alive in the least, for my students or for me. What I had originally wanted to do more than anything else had been forgotten. Joy had been sold for thirty quiet students and here I was, standing in Room 24, crucifying the Truth all over again, my marker the lance shoved into Jesus's side. I betrayed the joy and fun I had so loved in college where I had learned the very subject I now taught. I'd reverted to the humorless, straight-laced, stick-in-the-mud me of my high school years, forgetting that dynamic joy and a positive disposition is so desperately needed to effectively evangelize.

LAUGHTER IN THE HALLS

Diagonally across from my classroom is Room 26, a large, win-dowed room occupied by the effervescent and ever-engaging Mr. Robbie Austin, an artist by training and a theology teacher by God's design. Mr. Austin began teaching sophomore the-ology at St. Louis when I was a junior, which meant I was lucky enough to know who he was, but unlucky enough to have never had his class. I often wonder if he had taught me the stick I had forcefully lodged in the mud would've been pulled up a little sooner. Mr. Austin is one of those teachers a student doesn't easily forget. He wore cuffed pants with crazy socks and told stories about seeming nonsense that somehow connected back to the original theological point he intended to make. Add creative facial hair, a shark-fin Mohawk on top of his head, and a unique screeching shout to say hello to faculty and students each morning, and you've got the most unique guy in the entire school, maybe the whole town. And there he was, a stone's throw from my classroom door with laughter practically bursting out of the four walls encasing him and his students. He was beloved by his students who were simultaneously learning the material *and enjoying* the class. There was no overbearing seriousness or businesslike persona about him. Mr. Austin certainly hadn't waited to smile until midterms as evidenced by the laughter spilling from his classroom and filling up the hall.

Mr. Austin nicknamed me Monkey about two weeks into my first year teaching. I didn't have the heart to tell him I was pretty terrified of monkeys because he would walk into the foyer of the theology department each day and shout "Moooonnnnkeeeeeyyyy," the pitch of his voice getting higher as he hit the "eeeeyyy" sound. Most mornings he'd pop his head into my room and say, "Are we having fun yet?!" Then he'd bound his way over to his classroom and begin another day of his adventurous and excited teaching. After three months of using my efficiency-driven, serious, no-smiling methods, I noticed the misery that was slowly enveloping the cell block I foolishly called a classroom and I wanted nothing more than to be more like the mohawked teacher across the hall. So I began paying close attention to what Mr. Austin did every day.

Robbie greeted his students with boundless energy, even on the days I knew he probably wasn't in the best of moods. He remained professional with his students, but he wasn't the creepily mysterious teacher you secretly might think went home to sleep in a coffin with bats hanging from the ceiling. He told stories about his three kids and shared life experiences that were relevant and could teach a greater lesson. He wasn't afraid to smile, and he concentrated his efforts on making his students comfortable and happy, ready to engage with him and the material. Most important, Robbie made sure his students knew he wanted to be in the classroom with them and was having a good time. He liked what he was doing, found joy in the endeavor, and translated that joy for the teenagers sitting in the desks in his classroom. He enjoyed teaching, and his students enjoyed learning.

One Monday morning, after a weekend of putting together lesson plans and grading tests with abysmal scores, I trudged into Room 24 ready to begrudgingly tackle another week of boring teaching of my favorite subject. A few minutes later, I heard the "Monkey" greeting and the "Are we having fun yet?!" question ring through the department foyer, and overtaken by the desire to be better and different, I shouted, "Yes! Yes, I will have fun!" Immediately, Mr. Austin's face appeared in my doorway with a big toothy grin. "Good!" he shouted back. "Have a blast!" And off he went. As the first warning bell rung and freshmen began pouring into my classroom and taking their seats, I greeted and visited with the students, asking them about their weekend and telling them about my own. There was some confusion. Why was I talking to them? This was unexpected behavior from their no-nonsense teacher of the first three months of school. Usually, I was sitting behind my desk checking roll or putting an assignment up on the board. Now I was talking with them, even laughing. "Who is this and what have you done with Miss Prejean?" was plastered across their faces. After the morning prayer was finished over the school-wide loudspeaker, my well-trained and efficient students pulled out their materials for class and waited expectantly for the note taking to begin. Instead of opening with my usual "Make a new page titled . . ." I turned to my students and smiled.

Me: So I heard a pretty great joke a long time ago. Want to hear it?

Students: [silence and confusion]

Me: No, seriously. It's a great joke. Here goes . . .

Student A: Miss Prejean . . . are you okay? You never tell jokes.

Me: I know, but this is a good one, and I think you'll like it. My favorite professor in college told it to me.

Student B: Are we allowed to laugh?

Me: Of course. Tell you what, only laugh if it's funny, okay?

Student A: Will you get mad at us if we don't think it's funny?

Me: No! I'm just gonna tell it, okay? What did one monocle say to the other monocle?

Students: [more silence and confusion]

Me: Let's get together and make a spectacle of ourselves!

Students: [blank stares]

Student A: Ummm, Miss Prejean . . . what's a monocle?

While that first cheesy joke was a bit of a dud for a bunch of fourteen-year-old kids who had no idea what Victorian-era eyewear looked like, the ice was broken. I had wanted to make them laugh, I had cracked a smile, and the stick was pulled up from the mud and thrown across the field. Miss Prejean got her groove back. I began class every day with a joke, borrowing my sister's old joke books stashed on the shelves in the playroom at Mom and Dad's house. Storytelling became my standard way to explain theological points that I knew were complex and unrelatable. Practical jokes were frequent, including tricking my students into believing I sneezed so hard one time I busted my nose open when I hit my face on the board. The fake bloodstain is still on the sweater I was wearing that day. Every day, I made the effort to smile and laugh and try to put my students in a good mood before we began the lesson for the day. The same dynamic energy and joyful disposition I had and loved in college began to take over Room 24, and something began to change. Students were engaging me in conversation, entering the classroom with a story ready or a joke they wanted me to hear. I'd pass my freshmen in the halls, and they'd stop to say hello, looking for me to smile. I became less of a classroom dictator and more of a classroom cruise-ship director. My message became "Come aboard, and we'll do things together that will be simultaneously necessary for your education, enlightening for your soul, and uplifting for your spirit!" Room 24, or any classroom for that matter, didn't have to be a place of misery. Evangelization could happen and was happening in a dynamic way.

Slowly but surely, my classroom became a different place, a place where joy was translated in a visible way and began to reign supreme, thus changing both my students and me into people more joyfully encountering Christ.

LET JOY REIGN

Adopting and enacting an attitude of joy does not mean we are constantly giddy and ceaselessly happy. There were still plenty of moments when my students had to be corrected or I had to dish out a failing grade. No one is always in the perfect mood to evangelize, regardless of how fantastic your life may be or how strongly rooted your relationship is with Christ. But when we recognize that joy is an interior disposition that rises above the fray of the world, we are far more likely to maintain, live, and share the joy within us each and every day. Joy is the living of a life grounded in the Spirit and in pursuit of the will of the Father while delighting and resting in the love of the Son. Fostering personal encounters with Christ brings joy that is not easily shaken by external struggles nor will it disappear at the first sign of suffering. It is rooted in Truth and looks to the hope that endures in the promises of the Creator. If we truly believe in Jesus, both who he is and what he has done, and we want to share him with others, then joy must be the foundation and grounding of our life and the ways in which we evangelize.

I saw an advertisement once for the Dominican Sisters of St. Cecilia whose motherhouse is located in Nashville, Tennessee. The ad was simple: a nun kicking a soccer ball across a field, a huge smile on her face that lit up her eyes. I could practically hear the laughter as I held the magazine in my hands. Even now, having discerned a call to marriage, something about that advertisement makes me want to sell everything I own and go join those sisters. It would make anyone want to be there, which is exactly why the nuns use that picture to promote their convent. They know a secret: holiness is attractive, and joy is easily recognizable and actively sought by everyone. Spirited conversation, an inviting tone, billowing laughter, and a tender smile will set people on the path to meet and fall in love with Christ. When we evangelize with a spirit of joyfulness and witness to holiness with a delightful disposition, the Truth is more effectively and actively shared.

If given the choice to have a conversation with an angry Christian or a pleasant one, which would you choose? And who do you think is more likely to gain followers for the Kingdom, the fear-mongering, sin-shaming, hell-fire-and-brimstone believers or the charitable, welcoming, hope-sharing person who introduces the Savior who healed the sick, held the pained, and hung for every person on a cross?

We've all met them: those rigid, angry, "stuck in Lent" believers who aren't sharing a dynamic message but are instead introducing obstinate rules that seem oppressive and deadly rather than freeing and life giving. In fact, I'd dare say we've all met those people because we've all been those people a time or two. It's easy to become hung up on what we've done right and what others have done wrong or how we've believed longer and are therefore more worthy of calling ourselves disciples than the newbies who just now want to learn the Truth for themselves.

While the rules and structures of our faith are necessary and important, how we teach those rules and share those structures is key. All too often we focus all our energy on the stuff of our faith, becoming rigidly stuck in the substance, and forget the very people we work with and the Person we share. We risk becoming mere managers of evangelization, loving the structures we set up, and we ignore the people before us and the beautiful opportunity we've been given to joyfully and dynamically share Jesus.

In the course of evangelizing, we invite a person to experience the Truth, introduce and teach Jesus, and build a relationship with him or her as that person builds a relationship with Christ. We must do all of this with the joy of the same Lord we teach and share. If there is not a concerted effort to share the beauty of the Christian life and the love of the Lord in a joyful way, then our churches will be empty and stewardship lax. We'll see a shortage of vocations, students will be miserable, converts will be fewer, and the Church and her believers will be branded as rigid, bigoted nut-jobs. Oh wait . . .

Being joyful isn't just about getting students or new RCIA class attendees or parishioners in the pews or perfect strangers to like you and think you're a friendly person with a nice message. Our goal as we evangelize is to point to Someone beyond ourselves, and how we do that must reflect who he is and what he has done for us. The opportunities to evangelize, however numerous or infrequent, mean that we have the chance to possibly be the only gospel someone reads that day. We may be the only face of Christ someone sees, and the Gospel we share and the face they see needs to be one that doesn't have a sour look plastered across it with a mouth preaching a damning religion that has an angry, judgmental, boring Savior.

Our first task is to invite people to an encounter with Jesus, the seventy-times-seven forgiver and joy-giver. Jesus turns sorrow into joy. He fills the hearts of the apostles with joy, and he calms the worried heart with his unceasing love. As Pope Francis reminds us in *Evangelii Gaudium*, "Our Christian joy drinks of the wellspring of his brimming heart." If this God we share is a joyful God, should not we be joyful as we evangelize and introduce that message? Young kids learn a Bible school song that repeatedly proclaims this joy being "down in my heart" each and every day. We adults would do well to remember that the joy of the Lord should be the guiding principle of our efforts to evangelize. We must be a profound example of joy for those we invite to a relationship with Jesus Christ so that they can see firsthand that he will satisfy the deepest desires of their hearts and bring them the same joy that grounds and transforms our own lives.

CHAPTER 5

EAT, TEACH, SLEEP. REPEAT.

Student A: Miss Prejean, there's a lot less of you than there was last year.

Me: Ummm, excuse me?

Student B: I think he's trying to tell you that you lost weight.

Student C: I'm pretty sure she knows that; she is the one that lost the weight. It's not like it ran away.

Student B: Well, she had to lose it some way! Maybe she did run it off. Get it, Miss Prejean!?

Student A: I was just trying to compliment her . . . way to make it awkward.

THE BIGGER THEY ARE, THE HARDER THEY FALL

After graduating college in May of 2011, I moved to a suburb of Chicago to work in a small parish as youth minister. Cold winters, bland food, and the desire to live near my family eventually led me to move back to my hometown in Louisiana in the summer of 2012. My alma mater, St. Louis Catholic, had hired me to teach ninth grade religion, and my home parish, Our Lady Queen of Heaven, had offered me a high school youth minister position. I literally "had it all" in terms of jobs for a recent theology-major grad: teach by day, minister by night. Who wouldn't chomp at the bit to have two careers at once? So naturally, I did what any over-achieving, perfection-seeking girl who wants everyone to like her would do: I threw myself into my work.

Fancying myself a modern day youth ministry prophet who had come to bless my parish with my inherent knack for organizing Bible studies and planning pizza parties, I worked twelve-hour days all summer rebuilding and rebranding the youth group. We renovated the youth house immediately, adding new paint, rearranging the furniture, and establishing new open-house hours for teens to stop by throughout the week. Our Tuesday night Bible study grew in attendance, averaging forty teens within the first few weeks of the summer. Teens from the parish began signing up for diocesan youth ministry functions by the dozens, and as the high school religious education program kicked off in the fall semester, I knew our parish had found the perfect formula for youth ministry success, all thanks to my own tireless efforts and wonderful leadership.

When school began in mid-August, I added five eight-hour days in the classroom to my already busy work schedule. Being a new teacher, with no previous classroom experience,

I was convinced I could re-write theology curriculum for the better. I decided to ignore the textbooks they'd given me for my class, insisting that since they were the same ninth-grade religion books I had used as a freshman, they just weren't good enough. So I took it upon myself to reinvent the ninth-grade theology wheel, convinced I could teach my fourteen-year-old students the proofs of God's Existence by Thomas Aquinas, the attributes of the Church, and the doctrine of the Trinity all within the first ninety days of school. I was jetting back and forth from my white board in Room 24 to an ugly (but comfy) living room couch at the parish youth house. Mix in diocesan-wide ministry events on the weekends and the occasional speaking gig somewhere across the country, and I was convinced I had it all, could do it all, and no one else needed to get in my way, God included. Unbeknownst to me, I had the perfect recipe for a crash-and-burn disaster.

One afternoon in January 2013, while sitting at home grading a stack of tests, I took my usual social media break to peruse the postings of my friends on Facebook. The newsfeed reflected the usual: a friend had posted stories about her two adorable young children and their wild imaginations, people were up in arms about something President Obama had done, and my friend Brittany had finally shared photos from her wedding. I began clicking through the album of her pictures, remembering the great time we'd all had while gussied up in our blue bridesmaids dresses, when I saw the picture that tore down the ivory tower of busyness and success I had built for myself over the past few months.

I knew I had not been eating well, especially while I'd been in Chicago, and I knew it had been a while since I'd even come close to anything remotely resembling exercise. I had been blaming my diet of sodas and junk food on youth ministry, and there was no time to work out when there were lessons to plan and papers to grade. But still, as I sat there staring at the photo, I realized that I'd been blatantly ignoring how unhealthy I had become. I quickly clicked to the next picture, trying to erase the image of the heavy, unhealthy me from my mind and convince myself it was no big deal. There was no way I really looked like that . . . the camera adds ten pounds, right?

My parents had insisted I come over for dinner that evening, using the classic "you live in the same town as us and we haven't seen you in literally weeks" guilt-trip. After we finished eating, I snuck to the bathroom to stand on the ancient scale my parents had owned since they were first married. Despite the newer digital model scales my dad had tried to give to my mom over the years, she had always kept this one right by the sink, claiming that since it wasn't broken, there was no reason not to keep it. I wasn't prepared for the number staring back at me from the small face of a scale older than me.

173. One hundred seventy three. One. Seven. Three. No matter how it's written, the number stays the same, and no matter how closely I looked down at the tiny hands on the creaky old scale that's how much I weighed at only five feet, three (and a half) inches tall and twenty-three years old. The camera hadn't added ten pounds after all. My poor food choices, lack of exercise, and perpetual busyness had added the pounds, and it was far more than ten. As a young woman with the whole world ahead of me, professional success mine for the taking, I'd neglected one of the most important things in my life: my own health. I had eaten too much, moved around too little, stayed up too late, and paid attention to everything and everyone except my own wellbeing. I had eaten cafeteria food for lunch each day and plopped down on the couch and gorged on snacks after school before going to the parish to hang out with my youth group. I had spent my weekends on the road, eating fast food and grabbing sodas in airports.

I had let myself go and I had let myself down, all in the name of doing what I was convinced God called me to do. I was teaching fourteen-year-olds about the Church, I was spending time with teenagers leading them closer to Jesus, and I was traveling across the country sharing my stories and vision with audiences of teens and adults. This was my vocation: to build his Kingdom, to teach his Truth, and to form his people. But I was avoiding important questions: Who was paying the price for those long hours and that busy schedule? What else was over-extended besides my time? Sure, I could "do God's work" all day, every day, but at what cost? Who would ever actually benefit from an over-extended, too busy, unhealthy, frazzled me? The answer: no one, least of all me.

WEIGHING THE ODDS

After the rude wake-up call in my parent's bathroom, I went home and resolved to be healthier. I cleaned out my refrigerator and cleared the pantry of all sugary, salty, and fatty foods. I went online and began researching gym memberships in the area. I pulled out an old pair of sneakers and put them by the door and promised my dog I'd take him for a walk the very next morning. But the alarm rang the next morning at 5:30 a.m., and I rolled over and repeatedly hit the snooze button. The school day ended and I had a meeting to get to by 3:15. I didn't have time to go sign up at the gym four minutes away from my house. When my stomach started grumbling on my drive home that evening, I pulled into the first McDonald's I saw and grabbed a burger, scarfing it in the driveway because I was too ashamed to bring it inside my now foodless kitchen. Knowing the problems and even knowing the solutions were not enough—change needed to occur, for which I wasn't yet ready.

A myriad of other issues began to surface in my young life as well, and while the weight of gaining weight came crashing down, a lot of other things came with it. My prayer life was in the gutter simply because I wasn't committing any time to purposeful personal prayer. I knew the simple solution to this issue too: just do it—just make time to actually pray. I was also neglecting my family, seeing my parents only when I needed to drop off my rent check and texting my sister infrequently. I'd lost touch with close friends from college, missing weddings and the births of babies, barely even keeping up with them on Facebook. In the midst of attempting to achieve external success that I was certain was also building God's Kingdom, I'd forgotten to maintain balance in the kingdom of my heart in which he wanted to dwell. I had disregarded the most important people in my life, I was swamped with work, I was ignoring God, and I was overweight. I was blatantly rejecting the goodness God had given me, thinking I was choosing better things he would really want me to have if he was the good God he claimed to be. These were the problems in my life, each one staring me squarely in the face, ready to take a swing at my jaw.

Even knowing all of the problems I faced, I did nothing differently. Instead of recognizing my own failures and admitting I'd made mistakes and could use some help, I became angry at all the external issues I convinced myself were really to blame. I was angry at my teaching and ministry schedule, which was of course the reason I'd been eating such terrible food and had no time to exercise. I was angry there weren't more hours in the day for me to see my family or call my friends, certain that if I had more time I'd give it to them. I was angry that I'd never learned how to say "no" when people would ask me to do something, instead assuming the "youth ministry / teacher superhero" persona, thus running myself into the ground. But most of all, I was angry at God for calling me to two careers at the same time because this was clearly all his fault. Teaching and youth ministry were certainly compatible on paper, but my jobs were causing me more stress and anxiety than any twenty-three-year-old should have to face.

Anger consumed me, and nothing changed in my life except my mood. Instead of feeling tired and spent, I was now angry, tired, and spent. It became abundantly clear that my anger at all the external issues was really just the projection of the anger I felt with myself. I knew that running myself ragged and being so unhealthy wasn't part of God's plan. I knew that ignoring the people most important in my life was not what God called me to. I knew that early mornings and late nights in the name of productivity was not an excuse to ignore listening to the voice of the very God who had given me the chance to be so productive in his name in the first place. I was entirely aware of each problem, and I knew the necessary changes I needed to make to fix each one. But therein was the root problem itself. Identifying the issues I faced was just half the battle. I needed to make the effort to enact the solution for each problem, and this would require working on myself before I gave my time and effort to any other thing to which I'd committed. I knew it would require admitting I needed the help of others and the abundant grace of God, two things which I'd been blatantly avoiding and rejecting because I truly believed I could do it on my own.

MY OWN WORST ENEMY

I'm certain that most of us get in our own way when it comes to recognizing problems and enacting solutions simply because we don't like to admit when we're wrong or that we're incapable of doing everything on our own. We blame and make excuses and pinpoint external factors that "forced" us into failure. It's simply our pride getting in the way, something that the human race has faced from the dawn of creation.

Despite being surrounded by the riches of the garden that God gave them, Adam and Eve were tricked into believing the lies of the sneaky serpent, lies saying that God was holding something back from them and he didn't actually have their best interests in mind. They were easily convinced that they themselves could be like God, forgetting that they already were made in his image and likeness. They quickly believed the threat of death was an empty lie fed to them by a miserly, dictatorial God who didn't really love them. And so, thinking they could become like God without God, they ate the forbidden fruit and usurped the authority of the Creator. Rather than trusting the One who had given them everything, they believed the great deceiver who convinced them to doubt God's goodness. And then the first creatures made in God's image and likeness couldn't even admit their own failures.

God entered the garden and began questioning Adam about why he disobeyed his one command, and Adam instantly blamed "the woman whom you gave to be with me." Breaking that one rule wasn't Adam's fault, oh no! It was Eve who made him do it, and it was God who gave him Eve. In his mind, Adam was instantly exonerated of all charges because of Eve's failure and God's very creation of her in the first place. And Eve couldn't own up to her own failure either! "The serpent tricked me," she claimed, hoping she, too, would be acquitted. Adam and Eve were too wrapped up in themselves and the sneaky lies of the serpent to even realize the greatest tragedy to take place in the garden that day: their blatant rejection of God's plan for them, all in the name of "we can do it on our own." Adam and Eve hid from God— literally by finding trees to crouch behind—but spiritually as well, hiding the shame of their failure and refusing to return to his loving arms. Rather than see the situation for what it was, identify it as a colossal mistake, and then instantly beg for God's mercy and forgiveness, Adam and Eve instead blamed and denounced and rejected one another and him. They were wrong, they knew it, and they couldn't face what they had done. The enemy ensnared them and turned them against themselves and their God, turning them into their own worst enemies.

That sounds familiar . . .

As tough as it was to admit then, and as hard as it is to write now, I had to recognize a few things that had manifested within me. I had become lazy, refusing to put forth any extra effort because I felt I was too spent in too many areas. I was arrogant and prideful, rejecting the help of others and God. I was unwilling to make any sort of sacrifices to do better in my own life and live up to God's true call for me, instead claiming I could *do it all* without ever *being with* the One who called me to do it. In short, I wasn't ready to get over myself and do what I knew needed to be done. I wasn't ready to crawl back to God and admit I needed his help. Despite having jobs that focused on things about God, I wanted nothing to do with God himself for fear that he would point out the areas he and I needed to work on. I wasn't ready to surrender and recognize that I couldn't teach, share, or give what I myself did not have. I had found my own trees to crouch behind. I was hiding from God, blaming everyone else and even him for the problems I faced. I was blatantly rejecting the wellspring of love, mercy, and grace waiting for me. I, too, had turned into my own worst enemy, no better than Adam and Eve standing ashamed and naked in a garden.

THE TURNING POINT

Just a few months after the fateful evening when my weight, and every other problem, came crashing down, I found myself scrolling through Facebook on yet another evening of grading tests and writing lesson plans. A friend had posted a picture of herself in a Target dressing room with the caption, "Down from size 12 to 6: half the size and feeling great!" I hadn't seen her in a while and had no idea she'd been working out and losing weight. But there she was, a big smile across her face, wearing a pair of cute pants and an adorable blouse that fit her in just the right way. I pathetically thought to myself, "It must be nice to be that thin, why can't I be like that?"

And then it hit me: the only person keeping me from looking and feeling that way was myself. After months, years even, of being an over-worked, over-stressed, personally lazy bum, I had become aware of what needed to be done and simply refused to do it. Instead, I had hidden. Instead, I had blamed. Instead, I had made countless excuses instead of turning to the One who made me in his image and crying out for his forgiveness and help. I sat on my couch staring at the picture of my newly thin friend, and I began to cry.

I had failed. I had allowed myself to get to this point in my life, and I had removed myself from the one Person who wanted to take care of every problem for me. I had rejected his love in the name of working for him and, in the process, had destroyed any real chance of knowing him myself. Teaching Jesus to others and serving in his name would only ever truly work if I was first taking care of myself. After sitting on my couch and weeping for longer than I care to admit, I made a resolution: I was going to get back on track. I was going to fix my prayer life, I was going to get healthy and lose weight, I was going to refocus attention on my family and friends, and

I was going to learn how to say "no" in an effort to create balance in my professional life. And I was going to do it all with my Creator by my side.

From that moment forward, I would decide and do nothing without consulting God first. No food would be consumed, no words would be spoken, no time would be spent, no actions would be taken without first considering whether I was attempting to fulfill God's will or my own. I wanted to be like him, and I was going to need him to help me. There was no way I could continue along the prideful path paved by Adam and Eve. I needed him if I was going to teach him, and I needed to trust him completely. I prayed a prayer that night, one that I don't recommend to anyone unless there is absolute readiness for God to completely break walls and build bridges within your life. I sat on my couch, tears freely flowing, and whispered, "God, I give you permission to remove anyone or anything from my life that is keeping me from being the best version of myself. Bring me closer to your heart. Make me holy. Put in my life whatever will get me closer to you."

I slowly began to create a routine for myself that included daily prayer, portion controlled and healthier meals, daily workouts and physical activity, and equal time for both work and play with family and friends. Very slowly, as my pride subsided and my awareness of my need for God increased, I began to wake up more and more excited for each new day. I was ready to tackle challenges, not because I knew I could be successful but because I knew God would equip me with his power to work and serve in his name. I decided to re-read the gospels from the beginning, and it was like I was meeting Jesus for the first time all over again. I began to make attendance at daily Mass a top priority for myself. I started having dinner with my parents every week and would consciously call my sister and grandparents for longer than three or four minutes at a time. I started to build friendships that became some of the deepest and most cherished I could've hoped for, and I forced myself to join a gym and go work out every single day.

The change in my weight and attitude became glaringly obvious. I had been a heavy girl: physically, emotionally, spiritually, socially. In every area of my life I had been carrying around too much weight. I'll say that again: I was carrying around too much weight. Me. Katie. On my own. *I* was carrying the weight. I was prideful as I carried the worries of my life. I was identifying problems and recognizing solutions and never following through because I, a sinful, prideful, too busy human, was getting in my own way and rejecting the love and help of the God who made me. I clung to control and focused on fulfilling my own will and, in the process, hurt myself more than if I had surrendered to the all-good will of God in the first place. I believed myself to be invincible and untiring instead of acknowledging that I must first take care of myself, with God, in order to fulfill his will.

GIVE WHAT YOU HAVE

After stepping off the scale in my parent's bathroom on that fateful evening, I walked back into the kitchen to help my dad do the dishes. While standing there with a towel, drying the pots and pans mom had used to make her famous meatloaf, my dad struck up conversation, asking me how things were going at school. He asked if I still liked being in both the classroom and in a parish position. I answered his questions slowly, almost too tired to talk. After five minutes of painful dialogue, he turned off the water from the sink and turned to look me square in the eye. "Katie-bug," he said, "I'm worried about you. You're working too hard, you're moving too fast, and you're shutting everyone out. You're running on fumes, and you can't give what you don't have. Take some time for yourself, okay? Take care of yourself so God can use more of you in the right way, all right? Promise me."

I had gradually convinced myself that focusing on everything around me and ignoring myself would make me the most successful teacher and minister the Church had ever seen. Isn't this what God wanted from me? To serve him endlessly at all costs? I was called to "do something" for God because that's what he needs! He needs builders of kingdoms and workers in the vineyard! He needs a tiller of the garden and a teacher of his Truth! But I learned, very slowly and in more ways than one, that to effectively serve and build for God required also taking care of myself. Otherwise he would gain nothing more than a tired, ineffective, prideful servant.

How often do we run ourselves into the ground and cling to our burdens rather than cast them on the Lord, who assures us he will sustain us in times of trouble (see Ps 55:22)? Why do we sit around anxious about tomorrow, spending countless hours on lesson plans and meeting agendas while forgetting that God takes care of the littlest sparrows, meaning he will of course be mindful of us (see Mt 6:26)? How frequently do we forget that we are the beloved creatures of a God who can control even the mighty winds of turbulent storms with just the words, "Peace. Be still" (see Mk 4:39)? Why do we ignore Jesus' reminder that while yes, the world is full of trials and tribulations, he has already conquered the world and we are called to share in his victory (see Jn 16:33)?

If we want to effectively evangelize in our schools, parishes, offices, and amongst our family and friends, our own cups must runneth over and our own tanks must be full before we can try to influence anyone else. Working for the Lord isn't always easy. There's always a meeting to attend, a lesson to plan and teach, a game to run with teenagers, and a refrigerator with moldy cheese from last year sticking to the door. There is always an excuse for why we're too busy to do this or that, why we're unavailable for so-and-so and such-and-such, because our busy-ness for God is the best kind of busy to be, right?

There is no doubt God wants us to work for his greater glory and serve in his name. In fact, it is the greatest joy of our lives to have the chance to share the Truth and bring others closer to his heart. But even God rested on the seventh day. Even Jesus went off by himself to pray and reflect. Even the vineyard owner let the workers leave the field at five o'clock. Effective evangelization can only occur when the evangelizer is being affected themselves by the very same God he or she is sharing. It is a challenging task to give what we have received because too often we forget to receive him for ourselves. We struggle to strike a balance, which is often hard to initially find, and then quickly lose it.

Our cups are filled from a faucet and then poured out into a bowl, and while those around us benefit from the service and time and ministry we have so joyfully and busily given, we ourselves are empty. But what if we placed the cup into the bowl and moved the bowl and cup into the sink together and turned the faucet on? As the cup is filled with water, the bowl is then filled with the overflowing water pouring from the cup. There is a simultaneous receiving and giving: both the evangelized and the evangelizer benefit. In this scenario, there is no exhaustive expense of energy without a chance to refuel. There is no chance to fiercely control schedules and ignore God's greater will. There's no shameful hiding and prideful blaming. In this scenario, when those of us called to evangelize receive God's grace and simultaneously share what we have received, there are abundant opportunities to effectively and joyfully give what we ourselves have been given.

CHAPTER 6

CUTE SHOES

Student A: Miss Prejean, I like your orange and blue dress. It's super cute.

Me: Well, thank you. It was the only clean thing I had in my closet this morning. I haven't done laundry in a while.

Student B: You should avoid washing clothes more often then because that's the best outfit you've worn all year.

THEY'RE ALWAYS WATCHING

Every morning I enter school through the same door and walk down a locker-lined hallway with students standing and sitting on either side. Twenty seconds of quick head nods and "Hello, good mornings" later, I make my way across the commons area filled with students, teachers, coaches, and occasionally parents, with a heavy bag of books and papers slung across my shoulder and a half-empty travel mug in my hand. I hurriedly enter the theology department, conveniently located in the center of the school, throw my stuff down in my classroom, turn on my laptop at my desk, and then walk the hundred steps over to the main office to sign in, refill my mug with hot coffee, and check my mailbox. It's a simple routine, boring to even type out, but every step of the way, I know I'm being noticed and watched by the students lining the halls, leaning against lockers, and sitting on benches.

High school students, especially freshmen girls, notice everything, from how many times you've walked into the office in the morning to refill your coffee cup to the number of days in a row you've worn the same pair of shoes. Something about those adolescent years inspires fine-tuned observation skills that are used more on the teachers standing in the front of classrooms than on anyone else, except maybe their fellow teenagers. Wardrobe, tone of voice, facial expressions, body posture, mood, even the number of times a specific topic is brought up in a conversation—all of it is noted and the information added to the file each student keeps in his or her brain about that specific teacher. Teenagers aren't as unaware and clueless as we sometimes think they are. In fact, I'd dare say they're paying more attention and noticing tiny details far more than most adults on any given day. When the greatest crisis of their day is the five extra minutes it took their best friend to text them back, they have ample amounts of time to spend analyzing, critiquing, and noticing every single thing the people around them do, especially paying attention to the adults they have to spend five days a week with in the close quarters of classrooms.

I never really knew how much my students paid attention to what I did until my second year of teaching. In early October, a student walked into my classroom after lunch and asked, "Miss Prejean, did you not get to eat lunch today?" I explained to her that I didn't have time to eat since I had some papers that had to be graded by three o'clock, and I didn't want to fall behind by taking a break. "How'd you know I didn't have lunch?" I asked her. "Oh," she said casually as she sat down in her desk, "I noticed you didn't walk to the office with your Tupperware to heat up your soup, so I was just curious. I hope you're not too grumpy since you didn't get to eat." She had no idea that she'd just let it slip that she knew exactly what I did at 11:40 a.m. each day, not to mention that she also knew I usually had a Tupperware container of soup to eat. I didn't know whether I should be creeped out or flattered.

As class began, it occurred to me that if my students noticed my daily routine at lunchtime, then they certainly had to be aware of other things. Had they noticed that every Tuesday I wore the same pair of blue pants, worn for comfort as I went from teaching to leading my parish Bible study? Had they noticed I sometimes wore those pants two days in a row? Did they notice that I had gotten a haircut just a few weeks before but still continued to pull my frizzy red hair back into a ponytail because it was always unruly no matter how short I had it cut? Had they picked up on my favorite TV shows or what kind of music I liked in the course of our conversations and class lectures? Had they noticed that on Fridays I usually wore a dress because we had Mass as a school community but that I never wore high heels because I was too clumsy to walk in them? Did they know the name of my dog or what kind of car I drove? Did they notice how frequently I would check my phone while sitting at my desk if they were working on an assignment? Had they noticed that conversations with particular coworkers put me in a foul mood or that certain students knew just how to tick me off? Did they know what made me laugh or how easy it was to get me off track in the middle of a lecture just by laughing at a cheesy comment I'd made? Did they know what frustrated me and how hot-headed I could be if a student was particularly annoying? Did they know my favorite books of scripture or anything about my relationship with Christ? Had they seen me pray and did they know anything, even if just a little bit, about my personal faith journey?

The questions bouncing around in my head began to bother me, especially the last two about prayer and my faith journey. I knew that I had certainly taught my students plenty about the Catholic faith and Jesus Christ. My midterm exam and end of the year project were becoming legendary in the school. My students were taking copious notes and completing plenty of homework and most of them could carry on an intelligent conversation about a variety of issues concerning the Church. I knew I had even engaged with many of them personally, attempting to make them comfortable by joyfully and specifically paying attention to their lives, attending their ballet recitals, participating in the class skits for homecoming week, and occasionally going over to their homes for dinner with their parents.

But had I been so focused on noticing them that I'd forgotten that they were noticing me, too? It dawned on me that saying things about Jesus and giving lectures about the faith were only small parts of my job. Was I—one of the people charged with my students' spiritual formation—myself living those teachings of Jesus and witnessing to the faith I taught?

UNPLANNED LESSONS

After making a Lenten commitment to spend a few minutes in prayer at the beginning of each school day, I'd gotten into the habit of popping into the chapel before the first bell rang each morning. Students would be seated all around the commons, some propped against lockers diligently finishing assignments and others clumped together at tables in the cafeteria or on benches as I walked over to the small, round chapel. Although it has since been renovated, then it left a lot to be desired by way of liturgical esthetic. It had '70s style green carpet, a frequently empty holy water font, and faded bricked siding that morphed into floppy brown accordion walls that were opened on Fridays to transform the commons into a church. Despite its needed improvements, I loved our small chapel in the center of the school. I still do. It is simple and homey, familiar and welcoming, and it of course has Christ present in the Blessed Sacrament reserved in the tabernacle, making it the most important place on campus. The lack of extravagance in the chapel is somewhat refreshing and honest. It isn't trying to be anything other than a small refuge in the middle of the school, an oasis of calm in the sea of dramatic, loud, boisterous teenagers. Christ dwells there and all are welcome to find rest within.

Every once in a while a few others would be in the chapel on those Lent mornings. The Students for Life group prayed the Rosary once a month before school began and for a few Friday mornings one month the chaplain celebrated the Rite of Eucharistic Exposition and Benediction, which attracted at least a dozen students. But most mornings, the chapel was empty. Students were getting ready for their day, finishing homework and catching up with their friends. I couldn't blame them for not giving up their precious final minutes of unscheduled time, plus, it meant I'd get to escape into the chapel to just be alone with Jesus. No one would bother me in there, giving me a few moments of peace and quiet before the chaos of the day began. While the noise of students in the commons surrounded the small chapel, the sounds were muted as soon as I entered in. I'd genuflect, grab the prayer book I kept on the bottom shelf of the credence table, and take a seat in one of the wooden chairs against the back wall. Ten to fifteen minutes in the chapel was just enough time to settle my restless heart and calm my often-confused soul. Whether I had a bone to pick about a student or just needed to rest in his presence, my few minutes with Jesus first thing in the morning were the boost I needed to walk into the day with a positive attitude and the spirited confidence to effectively evangelize and teach.

On a typical Tuesday, as I hurriedly rushed into the chapel with only five minutes before the bell was set to ring, I was startled to find a young lady kneeling in front of the tabernacle clutching a rosary in her hands. Her eyes were closed and the sounds of students spilled into the quiet chapel as I opened the door and slipped into my usual chair. She turned around, smiled, and then continued her prayers. She was a senior, a lovely, energetic, charming young lady named Sue who'd been on the homecoming court that year and was involved in many clubs on campus. I'd never seen her in the chapel before, but I knew she was one of the more prayerful students at Mass on Fridays and had seen her active involvement in various youth ministry groups in the diocese. She was perfectly still as she knelt in front of the tabernacle, her mouth moving quickly as she silently recited the words of the "Hail, Holy Queen," finishing right as the first bell rang. She popped up, turned around and waved as she cheerfully whispered, "Bye, Miss Prejean. Cute shoes! I like how they match the color of your shirt. Have a good day!" and she bounded out of the chapel, going off to her first period class. I looked down at my shoes, surprised she even saw them.

From that day on, Sue was in the chapel every morning, always kneeling in front of the tabernacle with her rosary. And every morning, she'd smile and whisper "Bye, Miss Prejean" before jetting out the door and back into the bustle of the commons. Two weeks after our first encounter in the chapel, she walked into my classroom before school began.

"I noticed you weren't in the chapel today," she said.

"Yeah, I had a parent-teacher conference this morning that ran a little long. How was Jesus?" I asked.

"Great, as usual. Holy and divine and all . . ." Sue said. She looked excitedly around the classroom, her voice hitting a high-pitched level as she hurriedly said, "I wanted to let you know that I finished my fifty-four day Rosary novena this morning. I've been praying the novena with the specific intention of the discernment of my vocation."

I told her I thought that was a great endeavor to have undertaken and that I was proud of her for sticking out the full fifty-four days. I was curious, though. "Sue, I noticed you were in the chapel praying the Rosary only the last couple of weeks. Why'd you all of a sudden want to pray in there if you've been doing the novena for a few weeks before that?" I asked

She looked down sheepishly at the floor. "Can I be honest, Miss Prejean?"

"Of course," I reassured her.

"I've noticed for a while that you go into the chapel each morning, and I've always been kind of jealous of you. You're so confident just walking across the commons and going into the chapel, not really caring if anyone sees you or what they'll think about you if you do go in there."

"I'm a religion teacher, Sue, what do they expect!" I jokingly said. I was puzzled by what she'd told me, though. I hadn't realized students had noticed me going in and out of the chapel in the mornings. I figured they were far too preoccupied with themselves and each other to notice me.

"So anyway," Sue continued, "I decided that I wanted to have the same courage that you have and that I was going to spend the final two weeks of my novena in the chapel, discerning my vocation and asking God for the strength to stand up for and witness to what I believe in like I've seen you do."

I sat at my desk in stunned silence.

Smiling from ear to ear, Sue turned around and started to walk off. "Bye, Miss Prejean!" she shouted as she bounced on the balls of her feet out of Room 24.

Over the next few weeks, with her newfound sense of courage, Sue mentioned to a few of her friends that she would be in the chapel ten minutes before the morning warning bell rang and that they were welcome to join her. Slowly, more and more students could be found in the small chapel each morning, a hodge-podge assortment of kids kneeling and sitting on the edge of the chairs or leaning against the walls. Some had rosaries, others read scripture, a few just had their heads bowed with their eyes closed. But each of them, in their own way, were radically witnessing to their faith and relationship with Christ. I was in awe of Sue's invitation to her friends. I was even more surprised there were other students who wanted to take advantage of the quiet chapel's warmth and solitude in the middle of the busy commons. I honestly couldn't believe what was happening, surprised that a simple Lenten commitment was the inadvertent catalyst for students filling the chapel every morning.

I hadn't set out with the plan of "inspiring students to prayer." I just wanted a few moments of peace and quiet for myself, selfishly hoping to foster my own prayer life so that I could more effectively teach within the classroom. Effectively teach I did, but not in front of a white board with a marker like I anticipated. Instead, I'd taught not by giving a lecture and assigning homework but by walking across a crowded school and into a chapel, students noticing me the entire time. I didn't know anyone had even seen me going in there each morning.

It's not like I was carrying a sign that said "Please don't speak to me, I'm going to pray" or making a bold announcement of my schedule every morning. I just slipped in quietly, looking for respite before the classroom chaos. I never imagined my private chapel time would be as effective a classroom as the tiny, windowless room filled with desks and uniformed students.

So much of my time had been spent teaching in Room 24 about so many elements of the faith, and I would daresay some of it was valuable to my students. But a student learned far more from me because she had watched me walk to the chapel each morning. No number of well-planned lessons, meticulously crafted lectures, or perfectly structured assignments could replace the value of the witness I had unsuspectingly given. Not only had she watched me, she then wanted to do the same thing and invite others to join her. Sue was evangelized and then became the evangelist herself. Something had been caught, not merely taught.

A VISIBLE WITNESS

Seven years ago, the ACTS retreat movement took off in my hometown. ACTS is a lay-led parish retreat focused on adoration, community, theology, and service. The weekend retreat became one of the most popular, well-attended events many parishes offered, igniting faith and love for the Church across the diocese, the likes of which had never really been seen before. A small parish had been on the brink of bankruptcy. After hosting two ACTS retreats in the course of a year, the tithe nearly doubled and the parish grew financially stable. More people were signing up to volunteer with various ministries and many were returning to staff more retreats to help the movement continue. You could spot someone that had attended the retreat by the bracelet on their wrist, the bumper sticker on their car, and the enthusiastic back-thumping hug they'd give a fellow ACTS brother or sister.

About two months after I made an ACTS retreat, I put the bumper sticker on the back right corner of my vehicle, unashamed to share with anyone who passed me on the road that I had experienced the weekend and was changed by it. Less than twenty-four hours after the decal was in place, I was cut off in traffic and instantly let out a string of curse words and shot a not so nice hand gesture to my newfound enemy. No sooner had my hand gone down and my head stopped shaking in fury did I realize there was a cross with the letters *A.C.T.S.* stuck to the back of my Jeep. I shudder to think what that man thought of both me and anyone else who had that sticker on their car when he saw my rude gesture and watched the angry words pour out of my mouth. Sure, I'd stuck the sticker to my car but not much else seemed to stick after that.

In that moment, the concept of "someone is always watching" certainly wasn't in my mind. I had certainly forgotten that I had recently branded my car with a very visible sign that I loved Christ and wanted to live my life focused on him. I assumed we have to be "on the clock" to "do evangelization." But maintaining this mentality is nothing more than the limiting of Truth sharing to certain gatherings or specified hours in which to teach the faith. While scheduled times for formation are needed, whether they be in the traditional classroom, the adult education gathering at the parish, or in the planned "let me share my faith with you" dinner party with a friend, these are not the only opportunities we have to share what we love and believe. In fact, these are just the known, scheduled, "on the calendar opportunities" for evangelization.

So many more chances exist for us to be the visible witnesses necessary to boldly teach Jesus wherever we go and in whatever we are doing, including the moment when we're cut off in traffic and have a cross sticker on the back right of the bumper. Pope Paul VI made this need to witness very clear in the 1970s when he wrote in *Evangelii nuntiandi* (Evangelization in the Modern World), "Modern man listens more willingly to witnesses than to teachers, and if he does listen to teachers, it is because they are witnesses." Teachers teach, and do a good service, but our chaotic, noisy, secular world needs more than just diligent teachers. Our world needs living witnesses who profess belief through their daily lives, people who don't just tell it but show it. Far too often the world sees the inauthentic, dishonest believer who says one thing on Sunday and then acts entirely different on Monday morning. It's why Mahatma Gandhi said, "I like your Christ, but I do not like your Christians." The world sees rare glimpses of a person's life-altering belief in the Truth instead of the desperately needed frequent moments of authentic witness.

Our modern culture is one of constant chatter, never slowing down or silencing itself for even a moment. Twenty-four hour news channels, immediate answers to the most inane questions from Google, and instant access to the newsfeeds of our friends' lives keep us constantly aware of everything going on around us. As we stand in this chaotically noisy, half-truth filled world and look for opportunities to evangelize, we are called to make profound professions of faith and live radically different lives that *show*, not just *tell*, what we deeply believe and know to be true. There are enough teachers pontificating on television, clogging up the radio, publishing books, and wielding markers in classrooms to last every student, young or old, for a lifetime. We will only cut through this chaotic chatter with decisively different, brutally bold statements of faith that stand in stark contrast to the false truths that are whorishly bought and sold. We will only silence the noisy lies of secularism by *living* a life of faith, not just talking about it when it's most convenient.

Believing that evangelization will happen only when we plan for it—as if we are just teachers turning in lesson plans to the Holy Spirit, waiting for "You're good to share the Truth!" to be stamped across the pages—will only hurt our efforts. We schedule to give a talk at the parish RCIA gathering or we write the lecture for our students on the chosen theological concept for the week. We hand someone a book on a particular topic and hope his or her questions are answered in full as soon as the last page is turned. We invite a friend to Mass and secretly pray the homily is on point and relevant. These arranged moments are good and necessary, but we limit ourselves in thinking that our evangelization will be precisely scheduled and meticulously planned, and we forget something critical: evangelization happens less within the controlled environments of our own design and more in the spontaneous moments of our daily lives. Evangelization happens most and best when we live in a visibly faithful way. The faith we profess and Truth we believe must not simply be taught but also lived. We must be visible witnesses, sharing something by our actions more than just by the words pouring forth from our mouths.

When we constrict ourselves to scheduled teaching on its own rather than actively living what we believe, we can become blathering drones losing sight of the greater mission. We may fall into the trap of thinking that our scheduled teaching time is the only time we have to be faithful. Can you imagine if St. Peter had said, "I'm sorry, I'm off the clock" to the lame man crying out for healing? St. Augustine might never have become a bishop if his mother, Monica, had thought, "Well, it's Saturday, and that's my day off from praying for my wild child." We're certainly actively witnessing when we're sitting in the pew, attending the parish event, and lecturing in the classroom. But there is also great potential to evangelize when we're cut off in traffic, buying toilet paper, driving kids in the carpool, or responding to e-mails. Those mundane, normal moments are the ones when the intimate relationship we have with the Lord whom we've personally encountered is most needed. The normal moments of life are the ones that need the greatest witness to Christ. We don't necessarily need signs that announce "I'm sharing my faith now" hung around our necks or bumper stickered to our car. Instead, we simply need to become people of vibrant witness who visibly announce the faith in the humdrum, minuscule actions of daily life. We're able to witness in daily life and not just in the planned moments because the encounter we have had with Christ has changed us at our very core.

When our hearts have become his dwelling place and our wills have attuned to his, then we can live what we have read, learned ourselves, and taught to others. The words we speak become rooted in the Word made Flesh. Then we're not just talking heads with a pre-planned lecture. We're disciples with a story, an encounter to joyfully share in a loving way. When we've encountered Christ and fallen in love with him, the smile we flash at the woman standing behind us in the checkout line is a snapshot of the joy found in the Lord. When Jesus has changed us, the conversation we have with our friend about what we did over the weekend is not just a promo for Church picnics, but it is instead an exciting story of fellowship and good hot dogs in a wholesome environment of support, encouragement, and God's love. When faith becomes the rudder of our souls, we are steered in the direction of Truth, which then allows us to be the witnessing winds in the sails of others who are seeking the same fulfillment we have found. And that wind often blows when we are not expecting it to, driving

people to an encounter with Christ even while wearing a pair
of cute shoes.

CHAPTER 7

THE MIRACLE OF ROOM 24

Student: Miss Prejean, can I lead prayer today?

Me: Sure . . . take it away.

Student: Dear Jesus, we want to thank you for the play at school that I got bonus points for going to even though I didn't really go to it; I just got the playbill from a friend. Also, please let Miss Prejean stop being so uncomfortable when I hug her and help her become more comfortable when I hug her because I like hugging her. And, also, pray for Mrs. St. Cecilia whose head was chopped off. Amen.

PLUGGED IN

My first year teaching I had no official curriculum guide to follow. As I mentioned in an earlier chapter, the textbook was the same one I used my freshman year, eleven years before. The books were falling apart and the material was a bit out-dated, so the administration and department head told me to teach a basic introduction to Catholicism and touch on all the major topics pertinent to a mature understanding of the faith. I could use resources of my own discovery or design, and I could use the provided textbook if I wanted, but they didn't recommend it since we'd be getting new books the next year and I'd just have to change everything anyway. Basically, as a first year teacher with no formal teacher training, I was on my own. So…with the task of teaching an overview of a two-thousand-year-old religion in nine months with fourteen-year-olds who didn't want to be there in the first place, I determinedly set out to create something halfway decent for my first group of ~~guinea-pigs~~, uh, *students*.

I spent that summer re-reading books from college and formulating a sequence of ideas for the year. I scoured the Internet for resources and occasionally pulled out the dilapidated old textbook, looking for in-class work or pre-written tests. The year went moderately well; only a few minor disasters interrupted my plans. But despite my diligent preparations and what I thought was a well-thought-out schedule for the year, as soon as we returned from spring break in April, I was out of material. I walked into class one Monday morning, clueless as to what I was going to teach, hoping that inspiration (and a ready-to-turn-in lesson plan) would come down from heaven in the form of a very loud, booming voice or a hovering dove.

Inspiration came instead from a curious student.

"Miss Prejean, I heard something at Church yesterday that bothered me," he said as he walked in and got situated at his desk.

"Okay," I said. "What's bugging you?"

"Well, the priest was talking about that story with Martha and Mary, you know the one, where Martha is doing all this work and Mary is sitting around listening to Jesus talk."

"Yeah, I know the story. It's one of my favorites. What bothered you about it?"

"Well, I think that priest was just plain wrong. He told us that we should be equal parts Martha and Mary and we should work just as hard as we rest in the presence of Jesus. But, that's not right! I think the only way we can work hard is if we first just get to 'be with Jesus.' It's kind of like charging your phone. The phone won't work until you've plugged it in and let it charge. It won't do anything until you just let it be for a little while. That's how we have to be, too. We just have to be with Jesus before we can do anything for him!"

Another student chimed in.

"Or it's like if your phone is dying, you can still do stuff on it if it's plugged in, but it'll die if you unplug it! You have to charge it, and if you want to use it, you have to stay put in one place, just like Mary was just sitting there with Jesus!"

By this point, most of the students in the classroom were paying attention to the conversation. As I stood there, listening to my students continue to build on their cell-phone-charge analogy to describe the necessity of resting in the presence of Christ, I realized I had my material for the next couple weeks of school. I smiled and called out to my students, "Pull out your Bibles and flip to Luke 10:38–42, the story of Martha and Mary. Today, we're going to start a new unit on prayer."

A HOPELESS CAUSE ✗

My understanding of prayer had morphed over the years from one of childishly asking for things I wanted to the recognition of the necessity of frequent, personal communication with the

Lord. As a kid, I'd say my nightly prayers with my parents as they tucked me in. We'd pray grace before meals, and we'd frequent daily Mass when my parents were scheduled to serve as extraordinary ministers of communion or I was altar serving. It wasn't until I was well into college that I really began to understand the need for vulnerable honesty and intimate conversation with Jesus. In fact, for many years, prayer was very much a rote thing for me, something we were expected to do both at home and in my Catholic school. It was just another aspect of all the Catholic things we did, and I'd learned the hard way that sometimes it didn't necessarily go the way you wanted it to.

My sixth-grade year ended with my dad taking my sister and me to get Icees at the gas station before bringing us home to relish the excitement of a new summer about to begin. I couldn't wait for my mom to get off work so we could go to the movies, our traditional summer kick-off activity. But I immediately knew something was wrong when she walked through the door. Her eyes were red and puffy, as if she'd been crying, and she had a tired look across her face. Something bad had happened. Some terrible tragedy had upset my usually smiling mother.

"Mrs. Mary Vail has cancer, Katie," my mom said, as she collapsed on the couch with a long, sad sigh and began to cry again.

My mind instantly jumped to a fond memory of Mrs. Mary. After school one day, while a bake sale was being held at the carpool pick-up line, she'd snuck me a brownie for free, a twinkle in her eye. As she handed it to me she whispered, "I made this one special, just for you, Katie." That was Mrs. Mary in my mind: the mom who snuck you a brownie and told you it was a custom-made brownie meant only for you. She was the kind of person who made everyone feel as if they were the only and most important person in the room. She truly treasured her time with everyone she met, sharing her loving tenderness and kind heart with all. Mrs. Mary was everyone's favorite mom to see on campus because she usually brought both treats and a smile, both of which were immensely appreciated and enjoyed. She was a treasure to us all, a wonderful woman beloved by many. And now she was dying.

A heavy stone settled in the pit of my stomach as my mother gave me details about her lifelong friend's battle with the awful disease that was taking over her body. I instantly thought of my friends: her two daughters and son, Kristie, Allison, and Brandon. We were all growing up together at the time, hanging out at each other's homes and with each other's families, attending the same Catholic elementary and middle school, going to the same church and participating in the same youth group. The Vails were some of the kindest, most generous, and smartest people I knew. They were the kind of people you wanted to be best friends with, a family that had a deep-seated joy and love for God rooted in their hearts. No one deserves the tragedy of cancer, but this family certainly didn't. Knowing Mrs. Mary was sick just didn't seem real, as if my mom would snap her fingers and her cancer and pain and suffering would instantly be gone. My sixth-grade mind couldn't comprehend the idea that she was sick. More than that, my sixth-grade mind didn't understand how this was anything close to fair.

In a matter of days, the news of Mrs. Mary's diagnosis spread through the community. People began bringing meals to the Vails' home and setting up sleepovers so the kids had a place to stay when Mrs. Mary went for chemo. People chipped in hours of work to help keep the Vail farm operating while Mr. Mark cared for his wife. Flowers were sent, food was cooked, homes were opened, and in reverent and solemn tones across town, the mantra "Pray for Mary Vail" was said.

Mary Vail's name was on every prayer list in the diocese. Her name was said in the petitions at Mass, mentioned at Bible studies, said during grace around dinner tables, and written on the prayer wall at school. Mrs. Mary Vail had ovarian cancer, and the city of Lake Charles was going to pray her back to health, simple as that. It broke my heart to watch my friends deal with the rapid decline of their mother's health. Brandon, Kristie, and Allison weren't at school functions as much or regularly coming to youth group events anymore. Mr. Mark had lost weight (even though he was already thin as a rail). On the rare occasion that Mrs. Mary was feeling well enough to leave home, she looked tired and weak, as if she'd just come from running a marathon.

The cancer was brutal and swift, and in the fall of 2001, it was obvious that Mrs. Mary didn't have much time left. None of us knew what to do anymore. We had only to wait, all of us feeling helpless and useless for our friends in their time of great suffering. We all dreaded the morning announcements at school because we knew that one day the principal would come over the loud speaker and tell us all the heartbreaking news that we'd lost such a vibrant, loving woman who had been like a mother to us all.

In early December, while learning about the meaning of the Rosary and the power of prayer, my seventh-grade teacher, Mrs. Oden, taught us about the Novena of St. Jude, a powerful devotion prayed on behalf of hopeless causes. She told us there were numerous miracles associated with these nine days of prayer. I instantly had a great idea! When my mom picked me up from school that day, I immediately told her I knew how Mrs. Mary was going to get better. I was going to pray the Novena to St. Jude and, since a cure for her cancer was a hopeless cause, surely she'd be miraculously healed. My mom told me she thought it would be very nice of me to pray for Mrs. Mary like that, so she took me to the local Catholic bookstore and bought me the pamphlet of prayers for the St. Jude novena.

I began the novena on December 4, 2001. I prayed the prayers each morning, waking up thirty minutes early so I'd have enough time before getting ready for school. I'd say the Rosary every night before going to bed, begging God to cure Mrs. Mary and make her well. As far as my seventh-grade mind was concerned, there was no nobler cause for God to pay attention to and I was certain my prayers were going to miraculously heal Mrs. Mary. Every morning I'd excitedly announce to my mom and dad which day of the novena I was on, and each day I'd say, "I'm one day closer to Mrs. Mary being healed! It's going to work! She's going to get better!" Every day, my mom and dad would gently smile at me and say, "God's will be done, Katie. Just remember that."

On December 13, 2001, my alarm didn't go off, so I woke up later than normal and started the final day of prayers a few minutes later than I had been for the previous eight days. When I was finished I bounded downstairs to tell my parents that it was finally the day we'd get the phone call that Mrs. Mary was cancer-free and miraculously cured. As I walked down the stairs, there was an eerie quiet in the house. I couldn't hear the sounds of the *Today* show coming from the kitchen. My sister wasn't on the couch watching her morning episode of *The Andy Griffith Show* while she ate her bowl of cereal. Our incessantly yappy Chihuahua wasn't barking her head off, begging for scraps of my dad's toast. The only thing I heard were sobs coming from my parents' bedroom. I froze on the last step of the stairs.

My mom came out of their room, her eyes even more red and puffier than the day she'd come home to tell us Mrs. Mary was sick. My dad followed behind her, his face somber. They saw me standing on the bottom step, and my mom immediately started crying again.

Between her sobs, my mom slowly said, "Katie, Mrs. Mary died about a half hour ago."

My heart dropped as I sank down and sat on the bottom step of the stairs. I had started my novena prayers late that morning. I hadn't finished the novena in time. I was too late. I'd failed Mrs. Mary and her family. My novena didn't work. Hers was a hopeless cause, and I'd prayed the novena specifically meant for hopeless causes. But instead of finishing it on time, I'd accidentally slept in and hadn't prayed the prayers in time, and now, Mrs. Mary was gone. I sat there shaking my head in frustration and sadness. I'd done everything right and yet the prayers still hadn't work. I'd failed. The novena failed. The prayers failed. God failed.

When the tears began to flow, they weren't just tears of sadness. They were tears of anger. I couldn't believe God would do this, especially when so many of us had asked him not to. Did he just not care or pay attention? Did he really think it was right for Mrs. Mary to die, leaving behind a family and community that loved her? How could he do this? Did he not love her or anyone else? Did we mean nothing to him?

My seventh-grade mind couldn't comprehend the injustice of Mrs. Mary dying. It simply wasn't fair. She was the kindest, gentlest soul I'd ever known, and she had died from a terrible disease. But clearly God didn't hear our prayers or, and this thought was simultaneously scary and sad, he simply didn't care about them. Either way, I was resolved to never pray again. As far as I was concerned, prayer had just proven to be entirely pointless because after nine days of diligently praying for Mrs. Mary to be cured, she was now gone. I'd prayed for a miracle, wanting Mrs. Mary to be with her family and friends and community forever, and my request had been ignored. My prayer wasn't answered. My miracle was denied.

THE BETTER PART

I thought my prayers for Mrs. Mary didn't work and my request had gone unnoticed. My understanding of God was childish, ranking him with the likes of Santa Claus or the Tooth Fairy. He was just supposed to give you what you wanted, and just like I'd lost faith in Santa when that fat, old man didn't bring me an Easy-Bake Oven in the fourth grade, now seventh-grade Katie had placed God on the chopping block of belief. It should've been easy for God to grant my request, I thought, and so when it didn't happen, I felt as if I'd done something wrong. I hadn't prayed hard enough or long enough or I'd somehow chosen the wrong novena. I felt like a failure because it seemed as if I hadn't done enough for God to answer my prayers. Instead, he had abandoned Mrs. Mary and all the people who loved her.

I was making a critical mistake, of course, one that I still fall into even today as an adult with a far more mature understanding of God and his will. I was treating God like a genie who granted wishes instead of revering and loving him like the all-loving, all-knowing Creator of the Universe he is. When we treat God as nothing more than a big, blue cartoon character that emerges from a magic lamp to instantly give us exactly what we want, we become incapable of seeing, loving, and sharing him effectively. If we see him as a divine magician performing tricks to answer our every whim, our vision of God becomes tunneled. He becomes nothing more than a miserly dictator who either grants or denies the requests of us poor peasants banging on the palace doors. If God says "yes" then we've pleased him and done as we should, perhaps even believing that it is through our own merits and efforts that something has happened in our favor. But if God says "no" then we were ineffective and inadequate and God wants nothing to do with us. We become failures not worthy of God's seemingly limited love. Seeing God as nothing more than a gift giver also means that I thought of myself as the person who had to somehow get God to do something. I alone was responsible for rushing around in a flurry of prayerful activity to make God be God and do godly things. God's action was contingent upon what I did or didn't do. Rather than recognizing the free, unmerited gift of grace frequently bestowed upon us, I thought I had to punch a card and earn points to get God's gifts.

In my seventh-grade mind God was like a vending machine, which made me less of a beloved child created in his image and likeness and more of a customer who hadn't paid enough to get what I wanted. When we misunderstand the beauty, purpose, and gift of prayer, we completely misunderstand the power, desire, and love of the Lord. Our relationship with him will be impersonal and fruitless, becoming fleeting and infrequent because it is merely based on what we did or did not get. Without a deeply rooted relationship, our sharing of him will be feeble, lacking in the passion and vigor of one truly in love with Christ.) Understanding prayer and seeing God as more than just a divine sugar daddy is critically important because if we misunderstand the purpose of prayer, we will miss the mark in evangelization.

The story of Martha and Mary in the Gospel of Luke captures this misunderstanding perfectly. Martha confronts Jesus while he's spending time at her home, and she's pretty blunt with the Savior of the World. "Lord, do you not care" she asks

Jesus as she's running around the house. It's like she's saying, "Look at me, punching my card and earning the points to make you happy, and you're ignoring me while my lazy sister Mary just sits around relaxing."

"Martha, Martha," Jesus says, as if he's chuckling and shaking his head. He sees her punching her card. Jesus knows she's earning the points. But he also knows that in doing so, she's become "anxious and troubled about many things" and forgotten the most essential thing we all desperately need: relationship with him.

How many times have we prayed for a specific intention, planned and put on an event, gone out of our way to boldly share and witness to the Truth just like Jesus wants us to do, and it seems as if there's no fruit from our efforts? "Lord, do you not care!?" we cry out in vain. And there's Jesus, shaking his head tenderly at our misunderstanding of the entire point of sharing him in the first place: to intimately encounter him and vulnerably rest in his presence as we establish transformative relationships with him. When we evangelize effectively, we constantly point back to the person of Christ, emphasizing the necessity and importance of an intimate, personal encounter with Jesus that then builds an ongoing, life-changing relationship.

"Mary has chosen the better part, and it will not be taken from her," Jesus says to Martha. And what is this "better part" that's so much more important than the flurry of activity? The better part is resting in the presence of the Lord. The better part is "charging our phone" and "being still," as my students cleverly analogized on that Monday in April. The same words Jesus spoke to Martha about choosing the better part are applicable to us as we evangelize our students, coworkers, neighbors, and strangers. If we are teaching Jesus and stressing the importance of a relationship with him to others then we must first have that relationship with him ourselves. That relationship will only come about when we have personally and repeatedly encountered him by resting in his presence and allowing ourselves to both love and be loved by him. We can only be the Martha, doing the duties that are essential to the building of the kingdom, when we have first been the Mary, resting in his presence.

(This is the primary purpose of prayer: to intimately commune with God and vulnerably rest in his presence. Finding this intimate communion and resting in the presence of God is not easy and certainly not as handy as punching a card and earning the points or saying nine days of prayers to get God to do something. But that's not what prayer is meant to be. Prayer is not just a small percentage of our relationship with the Lord, something to be done only when there's a convenient time or a pressing need. Prayer *is* our relationship with Jesus. It's where we meet him, it's where we fall in love with him, and it's where we allow ourselves to be loved by him. As we enter into that communion, and allow it to guide the steps of our efforts to teach Jesus well, we come to realize that prayer isn't about "getting something" so much as it is about "receiving Someone." We come to see that evangelization, in a sense, is an experience of prayer. We're sharing the very same Lord whom we have intimately encountered, and in sharing him, we are able to encounter him even more. We give as we simultaneously receive.)

CEASELESS PRAYER

Effective evangelization begins with the extension of an invitation to an intimate encounter with Christ that then leads to a life-changing relationship with him. When we joyfully talk about, witness to, and encourage this intimate encounter, we must do so having repeatedly had those encounters ourselves. Our encounter with Christ is intimate, which then gives way to *continued* intimacy with him throughout the normal, mundane, daily routine of life. Prayer is not simply the recitation of words. Prayer is, most importantly, simply "being with Jesus" as we rest and rejoice in the presence of Love itself.

This is what it means to "pray without ceasing," words from Paul to the Thessalonians that are so seemingly difficult to follow. I can't pray a Rosary while I'm grocery shopping. I can't read scripture while I'm sitting in a meeting with a new client. I can't hand out holy cards to my new neighbor and invite them to pray a novena with me, a complete stranger. Well, I could, but a restraining order with the charge of "religious zealot" might be taken out against me. If we think of prayer as nothing more than the standard punching of a card and earning of points, then yes, ceaseless prayer is impossible for anyone outside the walls of a cloistered monastery. But when we see prayer as choosing the better part and we recognize and rest in the presence of the Lord whom we intimately encounter in even the most mundane moments, then ceaseless prayer is not mere activity: it is an inner disposition. Ceaseless prayer doesn't mean that our lips are always reciting the words or our knees are always glued to the floor. Ceaseless prayer means that our hearts are always united to his and our relationship with him is the animating force in our lives. Evangelization is not a scheduled activity but is a life lived in witness to the Truth. The charge behind this witnessing life is the continued, intimate resting in his presence—the daily choosing of the better part.

✳ ANSWERED PRAYERS

After being remarkably hurt that Mrs. Mary wasn't cured of her cancer even after diligently praying my Novena to St. Jude, I boldly told my mom I wasn't going to pray anymore. I'd cross my arms at the dinner table when everyone else said grace. I only mouthed the words at church and told my parents I wanted to quit altar serving. I was holding a grudge against God, convinced he'd just blatantly ignored my noble request for a miracle to keep Mrs. Mary with us, and I was going to give him the old-fashioned silent treatment for a little while.

After about three months, my mom asked me one day on the way to school, "Katie, has it ever occurred to you that maybe God did answer your prayer? Sometimes God doesn't do what we think he needs to because he has a bigger plan and purpose that we can't see just yet. Mrs. Mary couldn't be medically healed of her cancer. It spread too much and they found it too late, and that's very sad. But God took away her physical pain and suffering by bringing her to him in heaven. He did cure her, just not here on earth."

At the time, I just rolled my eyes at what my mom said. But as life went on and the pain of losing Mrs. Mary subsided, I eventually got over the fact that God didn't answer my prayer the way I had wanted. I began to think that maybe my mom was right after all. As the years went by, I all but forgot about my seventh-grade grudge against God and my novena praying for a miracle.

In the summer of 2012, when I signed my contract to begin teaching at St. Louis, I was told I'd be in Room 24, the smallest classroom in the theology department. It had no windows, notoriously cold temperatures, and a severe lack of storage space. But veterans of the department were well situated in all the other rooms, so I didn't have much choice as the newbie.

Room 24 was the least coveted space on campus, and I'd just have to make do. A few days before school began, I walked into the room for the first time since my freshman year to hang some posters and organize my desk. As I went to flip on the lights, my hand touched a metal sign bolted into the wall. A few years back, the school had undergone extensive renovations. Each room cost about $10,000 to renovate, so many people from the community had donated money in honor of alumni and loved ones. All the rooms had metal signs right by their doors with dedications etched on them.

As the fluorescent bulbs began to glow, I looked at the sign in my room and my eyes immediately began to well up with tears. In raised, gold letters, it said, "In loving memory of Mary Berken Vail."

The room I would be teaching in, where I'd spend most of my waking hours for the next three years sharing the Truth of the Faith and teaching Jesus, was dedicated to the woman I'd prayed to be miraculously healed so she could be with us forever. It had taken eleven years, and it certainly wasn't in the way I expected or imagined, but Mrs. Mary was there with me again. My prayer had been answered. I got my miracle after all.

CHAPTER 8

FROM THE FEAR

Student: Miss Prejean, you don't look so good today.
Me: Yeah, I'm not feeling well . . .
Student: Well, I was talking about your outfit, but I'm sorry you're sick.

THE DESIRE FOR BEING LOVED

"Miss Prejean, I heard you said in another class that dogs don't go to heaven. Is that really true?" It was certainly an interesting topic to kick off the class period, especially on a Monday morning after I'd returned from speaking at a youth conference the weekend before. I took a deep breath, thinking of how to approach a topic that was delicate and potentially confusing. I mentally said a quick prayer, something along the lines of, "Don't let me screw this up, Lord," before launching into the explanation of immortal versus temporal souls. It was a topic far beyond the regular scope of freshman theology, so I should've known that talking about someone's beloved dead dog wouldn't be a short or easy conversation.

A half hour into class, with some students clearly upset that I had just told them the chances of playing fetch with Fido while eternally worshipping God in heaven were slim to none, I finally threw in the towel. I held up my hands and harshly said, "Of all the people in this classroom right now, I'm the only one with a degree in theology and I assure you, I'm right about this. I'm almost never wrong, so you're just gonna have to trust me on this." Silence filled the room. I'd just played the trump card and not a single student could respond to my shut down. Technically, I was right: I did have a degree, I was more educated than everyone else in the room, and I was correct. But there was no need for me to say it the way that I did. In fact, I'd probably shredded any ounce of credibility by blatantly announcing I was smarter than my students.

The rest of the class period was largely uneventful. My students were quieter than normal as we went through the planned lecture material and assignment. No hands were raised or questions asked. I'd basically made it impossible for anyone to disagree with me for fear that I'd reference my degree again, making the whole class feel inferior and dumb. I felt bad for the way I'd handled the barrage of questions, and I knew I should apologize for snapping at them and shutting the conversation down. Something held me back, though. A small inkling of pride was running rampant, whispering in my ear, "Why should you have to apologize for being correct? If anything else, they should be thanking you for using your hard-earned, very expensive theology degree to teach them with a lackluster paycheck as your only reward!" I continued on with the lecture, the prideful thoughts eventually convincing me that I was God's very gift to my students and they were lucky to simply be in Room 24 in the first place.

The bell eventually rang and my students began filing out of the classroom. It took a few moments for me to realize it, but it seemed that they were all walking with a slight hunch, dejected looks on their face, almost as if they were kicked puppies left at the pound. It slowly began to dawn on me that my having to say that I was the smartest person in the room clearly meant I didn't think my students believed I was. But I wanted them to and I needed to convince them. I was focused on myself and how my students perceived me instead of concentrating on leading them closer to Christ and helping them understand the Truth. I ignored the fact that my students may have needed a better explanation, one that I, their self-proclaimed highly educated teacher, should have given to them. I disregarded the fact that they may have just needed more time to fully comprehend the material. I didn't even think about the fact that I was teaching on something that could be deeply personal and hard to hear. Instead, I simply spouted out facts and proclaimed my authority upon the topic as correct, feelings be damned. In my arrogance, I had merely climbed atop my high horse and proudly announced my credentials, thinking this would surely win them over to the Truth I was attempting to teach.

Arrogance and pride had blinded me to a simple reality: I didn't need to convince anyone of anything. The Truth can fight its own battles and will, in fact, win every single one. In the moment I declared myself the most intelligent person in the room, I was not teaching the Truth. I was merely attempting to convince my students of my own intelligence and theological prowess, and in the process of doing so I was actually inhibiting the Truth from being known. My students were not shown Christ in that moment in either the material taught or in the teacher teaching. They instead saw me, an arrogant individual witnessing to myself as I proudly held up an icon of my ego.

The whole rest of the day I felt queasy at the thought that I'd been the kind of teacher students probably hated. I was sick to my stomach knowing that I had given a weak explanation on a highly personal topic and decided to cop out of any deeper discussion with the statement, "I'm right, you're wrong, just deal with it." I left school that day knowing I should probably ask forgiveness for my pride and arrogance, and so at 5:15 p.m. I found myself kneeling in the confessional at my parish. As I listed off my sins, my voice caught in my throat as I whispered the last one: "I was rude and prideful with my students today, Father." There was a silence behind the screen and a few deep breaths before the priest gruffly said, "Well, that's not a good thing now, is it Miss Prejean?"

I hated it when he did that. The pastor knew my voice, and even if I went behind the screen to confess anonymously, he would still call me out.

"No, it probably isn't a good thing, Monsignor. I just got impatient and was sharp with them, and I should probably apologize," I sheepishly mumbled.

"I'd say that's a pretty good idea, Katie. You should also pray the Litany of Humility a few times this week to remind yourself that you are not the center of the universe. Throw in a few Hail Marys if you'd like, also. Now say your Act of Contrition, and I'll give you absolution . . ."

As I walked to the adoration chapel after leaving the confessional, I flipped through my *Handbook of Prayers* to find the Litany of Humility, a prayer I was certainly familiar with but often avoided. I was a junior in college when I first saw the Litany of Humility. My roommate had left a copy sitting on the kitchen counter, and I glanced it over while making my typical dinner, a PB&J with Ritz crackers and a glass of milk. The prayer seemed nice enough, but I wasn't particularly struck by it and didn't think anything of it as I went back to my room to eat and continue studying. The next day my systematics theology professor randomly mentioned in the middle of his lecture that he had begun praying the litany every morning before driving to work, to remind himself that he should be more patient and less aggressive about certain issues on campus. That same afternoon, I found a prayer book on the ground outside the chapel while walking into daily Mass. The bookmark inside was on the page for the Litany of Humility. I had now bumped into the prayer three times in twenty-four hours. I heard a message loud and clear: I should probably be praying the Litany of Humility.

That night, I printed a copy of the prayer and placed it in my *Magnificat* and began praying it sometimes before receiving Communion at Mass. I started to notice something odd. Within hours of praying the Litany of Humility, strange things would begin to happen. My zipper would be down or I'd get a parking ticket. A professor would hand down a less than desirable grade or I'd do something incredibly stupid and everyone would instantly find out about it. It seemed obvious that the Litany of Humility was a prayer that came with extreme consequences. So I began to avoid it. After only a few weeks of keeping a copy of the prayer with me, I stopped praying it for fear that the occasions for humility would continue presenting themselves. As far as I was concerned, there was no need to keep asking for humility because I'd clearly experienced it in full force over a short period of time. I had learned my lesson and convinced myself that more doses of humility would just have to wait.

Clearly the wait was now over after my dismal classroom behavior that morning.

The voice of pride began to whisper in my ear as I knelt in the chapel after my confession, but I was able to drown it out with the "From the desire of . . ." petitions in the litany.

I prayed the first part of the prayer slowly, mouthing each word quietly to myself. I prayed the litany again before going to bed that night and then the next morning before school began. As my students were walking into first period, I taped a copy to my desk so that I'd see it each time I sat down. I began class normally, with a prayer, roll call, and the cheesy joke of the day. I took a deep breath as the giggles died down from the "What do you call a fish with no eyes?" joke (answer: "fssssssshhhh").

"Y'all, I need to say something. I was unnecessarily rude and arrogant yesterday while we were discussing a very sensitive topic, and I was not a good teacher to you all. I'm sorry for the way I handled the situation and spoke, and I'm asking if you can please forgive me for what I said and how I acted."

The room was filled with a deafening silence for a solid minute. My students stared back at me like I'd grown a second head. I anxiously waited for their response, hoping forgiveness would be swift and things would be back to normal in Room 24. A student finally spoke up. "Are you serious, Miss P.? You're apologizing? To us? Teachers aren't supposed to do that." I stood there and nodded. "Yes, I'm apologizing. I was wrong and y'all deserve an apology, and I'd like your forgiveness."

The awkward silence continued for a few more moments before the students began calling out, "Of course we forgive you, Miss Prejean!" "Don't worry about it, Miss P.!" "We still love you. No biggie." Students began agreeing and nodding, and before long, we were launching into the lesson, my transgressions from the day before both forgotten and forgiven.

But something confused me. My students had been stunned into silence by the fact that I'd admitted fault. Apparently teachers weren't supposed to show weakness or failure. They had been taught that a student should never think their teachers were somehow wrong in the way they handled a situation or taught a topic. Teachers were to carry themselves as infallible authorities free from error or mistake, and if their students thought they were anything less than perfect, they were sorely mistaken. The fact that I'd apologized meant that I was probably the greatest teacher they'd ever had. Not only had I felt bad about the way I'd spoken to them, I'd had the guts to admit my error and ask for their forgiveness. I'd shown them my failure, and now these students probably loved me most out of all their teachers. They would probably be singing my praises to their parents and always think back to the moment Miss Prejean said she was sorry. They would come to me seeking advice. They would hold me, the most humble teacher of all who admitted her mistake, in high esteem.

Pride was sneaking back into my heart. So much for letting the Litany of Humility actually work in me!

BEING DESPISED

The rest of the school year was largely uneventful as far as my failures and apologies were concerned. To be safe, I continued praying the Litany of Humility every day as my students came into the classroom. My fears about the prayer were largely gone. Zippers weren't down, traffic tickets weren't given, and humiliatingly stupid mistakes weren't made (or at least weren't ever discovered). As far as I knew, I was as humble a teacher as they came. I didn't tout my credentials, I didn't say, "I'm right, you're wrong," and I didn't shut students down when they asked questions, expressed a different opinion, or attempted to correct a mistake I made. In my not-so-humble analysis, I was doing a fine job in Room 24.

As the school year came to a close, students began bring-ing me end-of-the-year gifts: coffee mugs, gift certificates, homemade baked goods, a chevron maxi skirt so I could be fashionable over the summer, and a lime-green beanie with the word "TWERK" across the top . . . the usual. One of my favorite students, a recently graduated senior, came into my classroom on the last day of finals and dropped off a short thank-you note in which she expressed her gratitude for the time I'd spent with her, the witness I'd given to the faith, and how happy she was that we'd grown to know one another. She had been a bright light in the school, a young lady who wanted to talk about everything from politics to my lack-luster love life when she'd pop into my classroom to say hello after lunch. Her constant energy, bright smile, encouraging and uplifting attitude, and graceful demeanor served as an inspiration for both her peers and me. The note she gave me was incredibly moving. In the midst of grading dozens of final exams, her short letter served as a much-needed boost to my spirits. It was, without a doubt, the highlight of my morning. After reading it a few times, I made my way to the chapel and said a quick prayer of thanksgiving for the gift of this young woman and thanked God for the chance to have been an example for her. I put the note in my bag and continued on with my day.

At about 1:45 that same day, with tests covering my desk and final grades due in an hour, another student came into Room 24. She rushed in, handed me a plain white envelope, mumbled, "Have a nice summer," and rushed right back out. I automatically assumed it was another note thanking me for the year, maybe with a gift card inside, so I waited to open it until I'd finished grading. An hour later, I opened it up as I was walking out to my car and began to read. It turned out to be far different than the thank-you note I was expecting.

Over the course of two pages, the student informed me that she hated my class, disagreed with most everything I had ever said, had no faith in God, and believed that her

open-minded opinion was far superior to my "limited, con-
servative, God-told-me-to-believe-this" teachings I had forced
upon my students throughout the year. My "anti-feminist, pro-
life, pro-traditional marriage" views were personally offensive
to her. I was "a poor example of a woman" who "had no idea
of what it meant to truly be alive," and I would, according to
her, one day realize that I was "buying into a belief system
that was made up by a bunch of old guys in dresses." My
"prideful presentation of ancient and outdated teachings that
have clearly been proven wrong" was "laughable, at best,"
and I needed to move past Christianity or I'd have nothing to
show for my life when I died someday because I'd "quickly
realize that heaven was just a figment of [my] imagination"
since I was "scared of death." The letter closed with, "You
always talked about Jesus and said he was loving, forgiving,
humble, and open to all sorts of different people. This year,
your class taught me that you, and most Christians, are not
really like Jesus at all."

Standing there in stunned silence in the middle of the commons, I re-read her words a few times, trying to process how
this seemingly quiet, never-disrespectful, always-made-an-A
student could have such a harsh opinion of me, my class, the
Church, and Christians in general. Tears began welling up in
my eyes as her words sunk in. As I looked up to make sure no
one was around to see my ugly crying, I realized I was standing about a hundred feet away from the chapel. As if almost
pushed (dragged kicking and screaming) by the hand of the
Holy Spirit, I slowly made my way into the same chapel I'd
been in just a few hours before. Earlier, I'd prayed in thanksgiving for a student I was immensely grateful for, knowing the
Lord had used me to help her and that he would continue to
do incredible things in her young life. Now, I was kneeling in
the same spot wanting to shake my fist at the tabernacle and

shout, "Well, you really messed it up with this kid, Jesus! It isn't my fault! You did this!"

As hurtful and humiliating as the letter was, the last line was the hardest to read. Over the course of nine months in my classroom, I had not been like Jesus to her. Instead, she saw me as an arrogant, self-righteous, pretentious, prideful individual who lorded my knowledge over her. Throughout the entire school year she had felt unwelcomed, unheard, and unloved. In her estimation, I did not live like the very same Jesus I taught. I had arrogantly considered myself God's gift to my students because of my education and mistakenly thinking I was exemplifying humility each day in Room 24 simply because I'd apologized for a mistake early in the year. In reality, I had fallen in love with being loved by my students and thinking they all adored me. As I read her letter, I realized that not all of them did. The chance to actually be humble and not fear being despised, ridiculed, wronged, or suspected was finally presenting itself.

After a few minutes of stifled crying and complaining to and fussing at God, I headed toward the door of the chapel. I noticed a stack of papers on the credence table, and as I pushed the door open, a breeze knocked one off. It landed right under my foot outside the chapel door. I looked down and saw through my tear-filled eyes the words, "The Litany of Humility." The prayer had finally struck again.

THE GRACE TO DESIRE IT

Acknowledging the need for humility is easy. Learning and living humility is certainly not. In the evangelistic mission, arrogance, self-righteousness, and pride—things that come natural to the average, sinful person—must be eradicated lest we destroy the work of the Lord. These attitudes do not ever serve evangelization. Instead, patience, understanding, and humility are of central importance when teaching Jesus and sharing the Truth with students, neighbors, coworkers, friends, or complete strangers. If we are anything other than humble when we evangelize and instead build up our own reputations then we will succeed in tearing down the Kingdom. When we evangelize and make Christ known, we must point not to ourselves but to him alone, and we must do so with the same humility with which he first shared himself.

Although it would certainly make for interesting illustrations in a children's Bible, God did not manifest himself by floating down on a cloud while shooting lightning bolts out of his eyes, though there are a number of terrifying moments in the Old Testament. Instead, he took on human flesh to redeem humankind, and in doing so, revealed his very self *to* the world while *in* the world. God chose to step into time as a tiny, helpless infant, weak and defenseless. And weak and defenseless is how Jesus chose to redeem humanity as he hung on the Cross and died. He was ridiculed, scorned, wronged, suspected, unloved, hated, and rejected. Jesus humbled himself to redeem us, and so we are called to humble ourselves and teach him.

The Word became Flesh and dwelt *among* us. Not above. Not around. Not standing on a stage at a podium with a loud microphone and a flashy PowerPoint presentation and an hour's worth of material. Jesus dwelt *among* us. He came to be with us, to meet us on our level, to find us on our own turf and share his very self, the Truth, and give us the Way so that we could have abundant life within him. If we want to evangelize successfully, we must model our approach after his. We must meet people where they are, spend time with them, and humbly share the Truth in a way that they can grasp. To humbly evangelize means we become instruments of invitation as we meet people, spend time among them, and provide opportunities for them to meet and fall in love with Christ.

The joyful witness we give and the relationships we build are in service to an intimate encounter with the Lord. As humble evangelizers, we should be pointing not to ourselves but to Christ. This is humility in its most concentrated form. We seek not to advance ourselves but to advance the work of the Lord. Our lives and stories should, in the end, draw others closer to Jesus, building up his Kingdom and not our own. The humble evangelizer is like the hired hand who plants the seeds that will then grow into a beautiful, fervent, blooming fruit. The seed must be planted, but it is through the efforts of water and sunlight that the seed grows, not the repetitive announcement of the hired hand's presence or the continued acknowledgment of the hired hand's hard work in planting the seed in the first place. The hired hand does the job and then continues to plant more seeds elsewhere. When we humbly evangelize, we play our small part, acknowledge God's greater role, and continue on our way.

It's no secret that humility is hard. More than any other virtue, humility must be wanted. It is not natural to want to be ridiculed, wronged, suspected, or forgotten. Called to the great task of evangelization, we pray for the virtue of humility so that we can, in some sense, keep our eye on the prize. It helps to pray for humility as we are called to go sit with the scorned sinner at supper, to take time with those who suffer as Jesus stopped for the woman with the hemorrhage, and to pray as we kneel to wash the feet of others.

To be humble does not mean we are weak or do not seek to defend the Truth. Ultimately, humble evangelization means we accept the moments of ridicule and misunderstanding. It means that we realize not every invitation we extend will result in the canonization of our next-door neighbor who joined us for the parish Bible study. The humble evangelizer points not to his or her own knowledge and understanding but to the great power, might, wisdom, and strength of the very God whom they are sharing.

It's easy to believe that I am doing a great service to those who encounter me and are then led to an encounter with Christ, and I often trick myself into thinking I am being humble while doing so. But I've come to realize that the moment I believe I am being humble is probably the moment I should pray for humility. As a pen in the great hand of God, I have to remember that I am not a number in the equation of evangelization—merely the plus sign. Are you and I essential to the process? Yes. Are we the primary focus in what is happening? Of course not.

As humble evangelizers, our role is to invite, to foster encounters, and to build relationships. We must joyfully meet people where they are, prayerfully engage questions, witness to the Truth we know, and beg the Lord for the grace to desire humility and do our part for his greater glory and for the mission to which we are called.

CHAPTER 9

STUMP MISS PREJEAN!

Student A: Miss Prejean, why aren't you married yet?
You're smart and pretty enough, I think.
Me: Well, I guess God just hasn't given me the right
guy yet.
Student B: That's a cop out answer! You have no
idea. . . . We totally stumped you!

THE OPPORTUNITY TO ANSWER

I was one of those kids who never really stopped talking. I
would ask questions about everything: "Why is the sky blue,
Mom?" "Why does the priest have to say those words, Dad?"
"What's the airspeed velocity of an unladen swallow?" (I went
through a brief Monty Python obsession in the fifth grade.)
My parents, saints that they are, would patiently field every
inquiry I lobbed at them, spending quality time teaching me all
the things I desperately wanted to know and even some stuff I
didn't. When my questions began to stump them, they would
respond with, "I don't know the answer to that, Katie, but I'll
find out." We'd go to the library or look things up online. My

parents built a home around the idea that we should ask questions and seek answers. Discovery was important, questioning was essential, and we should never hesitate to learn more.

Over the years, I was remarkably blessed to have teachers who fostered open, questioning, discovery-filled classrooms similar to the environment my parents created at home. My second grade teacher, Mrs. Tartamella, would walk around the classroom and ask each one of us individually if we had anything to ask her, and then she'd stoop down and answer the question right there with us at our desk. My fifth grade teacher, Mrs. Turnage, the sternest, toughest teacher I ever had, didn't tolerate back-talk and loathed laziness. But, if a student's hand was raised, she was at his or her desk in the blink of an eye to answer the question and give guidance. My eighth grade English teacher, Mrs. Ledoux, required each student to ask one relevant question every week to make sure we were checked in and on top of that week's topic. In her classroom, the asking of questions was a grade in and of itself. My parents encouraged my inquiries, and many of my teachers took the time to answer them, so I always felt comfortable with raising my hand and asking questions and seeking out an answer. All that changed when I got to high school and walked into Room 24, the freshman theology classroom, for the first time.

Excited to take high school theology, I was ready to learn about Catholicism and my faith, a subject I'd become enamored with over the preceding few years. It became very obvious very quickly that this would be a "textbook only" class, though. We completed worksheet after worksheet and planned five-minute prayer services that had to incorporate a contemporary song. We would spend an hour writing a weekly gospel reflection and turn them in for points, most of which we were never given back. I quickly became bored. The class was unengaging, the material was repetitive, and the teacher didn't seem to like us very much. Even as a freshman I knew that teaching couldn't be easy, but it seemed to me that if a person chose the profession of education then they should at least somewhat enjoy having a conversation with students and try to engage them with the subject. Occasionally, usually while we were completing worksheets, I'd muster up the courage to raise my hand and ask a question about something, hoping to get some sort of an answer. *The Passion of the Christ* film had been released that year, and I wanted to know more about the crucifixion of Jesus, specifically how he physically died. Politicians were throwing their hats in the ring for the 2004 election, and I had questions about abortion and other moral issues I was hearing about on the news. Mostly, I was curious as to why Catholicism was the one, true faith and why we considered ourselves to be the most correct "flavor" of Christianity on the market. But every time I raised my hand and asked my question, I was given the answer, "We don't have time for questions today; we have work to do."

I came to loathe that phrase: "We have work to do." What about the work of discovery? What about the work of inquiry? What about the work of actual learning instead of rote memorization? Isn't your work as a teacher to actually answer the questions I have instead of telling me to just go find the answer on my own, leading me to some deep, dark, heretical place on the Internet? Shouldn't our "work to do" be us engaging with the material and having thoughtful conversations that mean something rather than finishing word searches and filling in the blanks on worksheets?

My frustrations continued into sophomore year. My questions were getting more complex, especially ones concerning the truthfulness of Catholicism and the nature of God. My parents, out of answers and beginning to wonder about a number of things themselves, encouraged me to read and ask my teachers. A terrible tsunami and earthquake had hit India, killing more than two hundred thousand people and devastating the region. I couldn't make sense of how an all-knowing, all-loving God could allow such destruction and suffering. I kept pestering my sophomore theology teacher for an answer, convinced that I would stop believing in God unless someone could give me satisfying answers.

Annoyed with my perpetual hand raising and I suspect at a loss for answers, my sophomore theology teacher finally called in the big guns. She invited Deacon Glenn Viau, the academic administrator at the school, to visit our class one day and answer any and all questions we might have about Catholicism. I was elated. For seventy minutes, someone with good answers heard me, responded to me, and helped me understand. By the end of the class, I had more questions in my mind and couldn't wait for the chance to visit with him again and continue to pick his brain.

As the class came to an end, Deacon Viau said one of the most profound things I'd ever heard, words that endorsed my years of hand raising and question asking. "I want to leave you all with one thought," he said, a smile breaking across his face. "Remember, as a student, it is your duty and right to ask questions. Even if those questions are hard. Even if you may not want to hear the answer given or even if you ask it of a person who may not want to answer. If you don't ask questions, then the Church never has the opportunity to answer. And the Church can always give you an answer." After class ended that day, Deacon Viau invited me to stop by his office any time I wanted to chat. I took him up on his offer, eventually asking him to be my Confirmation sponsor and later, as an adult, my spiritual director. A simple invitation and the gift of his time were the catalysts for my continued discovery of the Truth and growth in faith. He taught me Jesus through the answers to my questions and in the life of faith he lived. He encouraged me to give the Church a chance to answer, and then did the important work of pointing me to and encouraging my relationship with the Truth.

WORK TO DO

After eighteen straight years as a student with a variety of teachers and professors, some more amenable to questions and discourse than others, I walked back into Room 24 resolved to be the type of teacher who never ignored a student's question or did not try my best to give them a satisfying, thorough, and correct answer. I wanted to create a classroom where hands were raised, questions voiced, and answers were given. I wanted them to ask the tough questions so the Church, with the fullness of Truth, had the opportunity to answer. I would be the captain of the question ship, steering my students through the murky waters of curiosity and bring them safely to the shore of answers. And then Hurricane Eric hit.

Eric had bright red hair, ivory white skin, and a shock of freckles across his nose. He was the classic, "I don't want to show you I care" student who came into class every day with his shirt un-tucked and an excuse for why he hadn't finished his homework, even though we both knew that he was the smartest one in the room. He was easily bored, not easily amused, a total genius who didn't want anyone to know he was so smart, and he usually slumped down in his desk with his arms crossed, looking bothered by the fact that he had to get up that morning in the first place.

But Eric was equal parts bored and curious in Room 24. While some topics didn't seem to interest him in the least, others would start a flurry of hand raising and questioning that would derail the entire lesson I had planned for class. And

I hated it. Sure, I wanted to be the exact opposite of my own freshman theology teacher and answer the tough questions that were thrown my way, but I also wanted to get through the material I'd diligently planned and which the school's curriculum required. It seemed, at times, as if Eric was asking questions just to see how far off topic he could get me. The day we spent nearly an hour discussing why Catholics honored saints knocked us off schedule for nearly a week. At other times, the questions he asked sparked great conversation amongst the other students, leading to a full class period devoted to simply going back and forth with Q & A on all things Catholic. Most times, he'd leave at the end of class with a smug look on his face, as if to say "I won this round, Miss P."

Two weeks before midterms and the Christmas break, I found myself scrambling to finish a unit on the seven sacraments. Anxious to cover the material which I'd already written questions about on the midterm exam that was copied and ready to hand out, my students came into class one day with the assignment to complete a worksheet on the matter, form, and minister of each sacrament. It was far more efficient to have them look up the answers in the textbook before giving a detailed lecture on the concept, so I gave them fifteen minutes to complete the chart before we'd begin.

A few minutes of blessed silence was interrupted by the oh so familiar, "Uhhh, Miss Prejean, I have a question . . ."

"Yes, Eric, what's up?" I tiredly said.

"Well, this textbook is talking about how the sacraments give us grace and that grace is how we live in the divine life of God, which is how you become holy and get to heaven someday."

"Yes, that's what the textbook says, Eric, but that isn't a question."

"So here's my question," he said, with an eye-roll so high I wondered if his eyes would ever come back down, "What about people who aren't Catholic and don't have the seven sacraments in their religion? Do they just not get grace?"

It was a good question, perhaps the best question he'd ever asked and one that I knew I could answer making reference to the many notes I'd taken on grace and the writings of Aquinas in my Apologetics courses taught by the estimable Dr. Malloy at UD. But it was also a question that would've derailed the entire topic for the day because it would inevitably lead to a discussion on the Protestant Reformation and the validity and infallibility of Catholicism, and I just didn't want to be even further off schedule than we already were.

I looked at him and sighed and said, "I tell you what, Eric. If we can take the notes we need to take right now and we have extra time left over, I'll be able to answer your question. But right now, we don't have time because *we have work to do.*"

A DAUNTING TASK

The day I used the excuse "we have work to do" to not answer Eric's questions, I spent the rest of the day frustrated at myself for not being better than the same teacher that had once ignored me in Room 24. Sure, we didn't really have time to get caught up in a conversation that was off topic, but I honestly could've taken just a few minutes to quickly explain the answer and then move on. I just didn't feel like taking the time, putting forth the effort, or going beyond the bare minimum in that moment. Eric had given me the chance to be a mouthpiece for the Truth, letting the Church answer, and I had squandered the opportunity in the name of "work to do." But what better work could there be than answering the questions of someone who is generally curious about a matter of faith, even if that someone is a student with a reputation for arguing? I used an excuse I myself had hated in the name of efficiency. I took the easy way out and ignored an essential part of the process of evangelization: taking the time to engage in meaningful dialogue to help someone further grow in knowledge and love of the Truth. I didn't do for Eric what my best teachers had once done for me.

After being frustrated with myself for missing the mark a few times and not taking the time to answer the inquiries of my curious, Truth-seeking students, I decided to try something different in Room 24. Inspired by students like Eric and myself who constantly raised their hands ready to ask some burning question that needed to be answered, I created a little game I dubbed "Stump Miss Prejean." I told my students to dedicate a page in their notebook to questions. Anytime they had something to ask, and if we didn't have enough time at that moment to discuss it fully, they would write it on that page. Randomly, one day a month, students would enter the classroom with *The Price Is Right* theme song playing. Notecards were passed out and a basket was placed at the front of the room and, for the length of the song, students could write any question down and turn it in for me to answer. The rest of the class period was spent answering the questions submitted and the many others that often sprung up as a result of the discussion.

Students began to look forward to "stump days," asking everything from "Why do you always have your hair pulled back in a ponytail?" (answer: because it looks like a small woodland creature living on the back of my head if it isn't tied up) to "What are demons and are exorcisms real?" (Answer: yes). The entire class would dial in, engaging with theological content they may have never really thought about but now had the chance to learn. The game was a hit and kids would ask at least once a day, "Are we gonna get to try and stump you this week?!" There was now a forum for their questions, and I didn't need to make excuses to avoid answering them. I made the time for dialogue and discovery, and it was one of the best things happening in my classroom. My only regret was that I hadn't created "Stump Miss Prejean" in my first year of teaching because Eric, the inspiration of the game, never got to play it. Not answering his question had prompted me to answer every other student's questions from that day forward.

I'd dare say many of us have skipped this "dialogue and discourse" step of evangelization plenty of times in our offices, homes, parishes, and neighborhoods. We convince ourselves that the simple invitation and the opportunity to encounter Christ is enough effort and we don't need to go any further. Perhaps the questions are hard to answer and would require far too much time. Maybe we know the answers are difficult to hear and are contrary to the thoughts of most secular minds, so we avoid isolating someone with a polarizing idea. Maybe we're not yet quite sure of the answers ourselves and fear we'll make a mistake or have to admit we just don't know. Perhaps we are just too busy in that moment and we think the question can wait. If we're being honest with ourselves, though, maybe somewhere in the back of our mind we're secretly hoping the question won't ever be brought up again and we can ignore it altogether. Whatever excuse we make for avoiding, many of us have somehow come to mistakenly believe that these questions, whether easy or tough to answer, can be swept to the side so we can pay attention to what we think are the far more important tasks. If this concept of staying busy and doing work simply for its own sake and simply to get by makes its way any further into our evangelizing efforts then we are surely doomed.

Oftentimes, under the guise of keeping busy, we've convinced ourselves that if we just do something that's related to sharing Jesus, regardless of what it is or whether or not it's any good, we are somehow evangelizing and that is enough. If we repeatedly do a lot of something, whether or not it is actually fruitful, then we're working hard and success will surely come. We slap a flyer on the parish doors and tell people we're having a night of fellowship. They'll show up, we'll serve cookies and punch, and BAM! It's the work of the Lord! We've done our duty and met our evangelization quota for the month. Rinse and repeat. Pass out a worksheet to keep the students busy while I grade the tests, that'll teach them the bare minimum of what needs to be taught, and WAM! Evangelization finished in the classroom today! Check that off the to-do list. But these lists of tasks and seemingly endless amounts of busy-work keep us from one of the most essential aspects of evangelization: personally dialoguing and spending quality time in conversation answering the tough questions about the faith that so many people who are encountering Christ will have, whether they are meeting him for the first time or in a reunion of sorts.

While engaging in this dialogue and answering these questions is certainly a daunting task that requires immense amounts of patience and charity with equal parts precision and clarity, the consequence of avoidance is detrimental. Should we ignore the tough questions, for whatever reason, we do a great disservice to the entire process of evangelization. It's as if we've invited someone to an awesome party and then left them standing alone in the foyer while we go find our best friends. Evangelization starts with invitation and an encounter that leads to a relationship with both Christ and others, but then we must welcome them into the family of faith and help them grow in knowledge of the Truth. We must spend quality time helping those who are evangelized meet, learn, and fall in love with the Truth. It is not enough for us to simply say,

"Join us, meet Jesus, we love you, and so does he." We must continue the conversation with, "What are you wondering? Where are you confused? How can we help you understand?" It falls on us to be the mouthpiece of Truth. The importance of answering the tough questions and engaging in meaningful dialogue cannot be missed for it is far too important to ignore in the name of "work to do." We are stewards of the rich, beautiful Faith we love and profess, called to share it with those whom we have invited to love and profess it with us.

As stewards, though, we must delicately walk the line between militant zealots who rudely pontificate and wishy-washy fence-sitters that lackadaisically give answers that may be nice to hear but are in fact wrong. As we engage in the dialogue that is so important to the process of evangelization, it is critically important that we remember we are evangelizing human beings. These are people, and people have thoughts. People have history. People may come into a conversation with questions they've pondered for thirty years or have preconceived notions about the Church they can't quite give up on just yet. Just as we invite others to an encounter with Christ with open, loving, welcoming arms, so too must the continued dialogue that answers tough questions be welcoming, honest, truthful, and charitable. Yes, sometimes charity requires telling a person they are wrong and then setting them on the right course. But even so, we must do so in the spirit of the always-Truthful but equally merciful Jesus. We must remain focused on *how* we extend invitations, foster encounters, build relationships, witness with our lives, and open pathways to honest dialogue for continued formation.

THE EVANGELIZED EVANGELIZERS

Occasionally while playing "Stump Miss Prejean" a student asks a doozy of a question that I can't quite give a thorough answer to, at which point the students get to yell, "We stumped you!" and are then awarded a bonus point ticket. This is everyone's favorite part of the game, mine included. Students get to feel smarter than me in that moment. Although I *am* the teacher, I do not know it all of course, and it is important for them to see that there remain many things for me to learn. I am certainly not the arbiter of all Truth or the keeper of all correct answers. I have much to discover. We all do. None of us will ever finish discovering the Truth, not until we're united with the Truth in the eternal banquet of heaven.

I'll never forget the day a student saw me sitting in the library studying for my graduate school final. Her jaw nearly hit the floor as she said, "You still have to go to school for theology! There's still stuff you don't know about God! No way." While I was certainly flattered she thought I knew everything, I made a point to let her know that there was still plenty of material I needed to learn. I didn't know it all, nor would I, and that was an exciting prospect because it meant I wasn't done growing and discovering yet.

Taking the time to engage in intentional question and answer time with my students not only benefited them but it also alerted me to holes in my knowledge, which then forced me to go ask questions and seek answers myself. I didn't like not being able to answer my students' questions, if for no other reason than it meant that they were left unsatisfied in their pursuit of Truth. If I was going to do my duty as their teacher, I needed to know the material well and be ready for any and all questions about the faith. I had invited them to encounter Christ, and I needed to continue the work of evangelization by helping them discover the Truth further. The only way I could adequately teach was if I continued to learn myself. If I was going to answer their questions then I must be asking my own questions as well. If I was going to evangelize, then I, too, needed to be evangelized.

At some point, our journey toward Jesus began. Someone invited us to encounter Christ and built a relationship with us. They hopefully answered our questions and radically and boldly witnessed to the Truth with their lives. Now we have the chance to do that for others. This does not mean that our name is then moved from a list of "evangelized" to "evange-lizer," and we magically swap categories as if to say, "They now do the work of the Lord and don't need anything done for them." If we think this, we are sorely mistaken. When we begin to evangelize, the importance of which cannot be understated, we do not just stop reaping the benefits of being evangelized ourselves. We simply become an "evangelized evangelizer"—one who does the work of the Lord and simul-taneously experiences the fruits of others' evangelizing work. Christ wants us to continue encountering him. It is not a one and done deal. We do not simply "get evangelized" and then move on. It becomes the very root of our lives—a cyclical expe-rience of inviting and being invited, of fostering encounter and encountering him ourselves, of being in relationship with Christ and others.

When I took the time to intentionally answer my students' questions and help them further discover the Truth, I came to realize that I had a lot of room to grow and so much more to learn. Sure, I was witnessing and teaching and doing the great work of evangelization, but I needed all those things done for me as well. As Christians, we have been entrusted with the tremendously important task of evangelizing in the mission fields of classrooms, offices, parishes, neighborhoods, hospitals, and any other place where a soul could be won for Christ. We should never think that we are "done" being evangelized as well. In fact, it is perhaps the greatest blessing of the one called to evangelize that they are surrounded by coworkers in the vineyard who can do for them what they do for others.

I LEARNED A LOT

Two years after Eric sat in Room 24 as my student, he registered in my parish's high school religious education program to prepare for Confirmation. As I walked into the room on the first night of the program, I saw him slumped down in a chair in the third row, his arms crossed and a bored expression across his face. Not much had changed. He was taller with fewer freckles, but he still shot his hand up every chance he got and asked questions. And I answered every single one. I was determined to not let them fall through the cracks.

I honestly didn't know if Eric would complete the formation and receive the sacrament. He seemed generally disinterested, just another teen forced to go through the program so his grandma wouldn't cry. On the night of the Confirmation ceremony, while students lined up to take pictures with the bishop, I walked up to Eric to tell him congratulations.

"So, do you feel any different, Eric? Is the Holy Spirit manifesting itself in your life right this minute?" I jokingly asked.

"Not really, Miss Prejean, but you told us we wouldn't feel it right away. The effects of the Holy Spirit will manifest at the most random of times, remember?" he said sarcastically.

"True. I did say that. Well, it was a joy having you in the program, Eric. I enjoyed teaching you again."

"You know, I enjoyed having you again, too, Miss Prejean. You're one of the only teachers who ever actually took the time to answer most of my questions. Thanks for that. I learned a lot."

CHAPTER 10

AVOIDING THE GREATEST TRAGEDY

Me: Okay, y'all, we have to complete these forms about your future plans for college and career so the school has an idea about your lifelong goals. I know it's long, but just deal with it. We'll try to do it quickly.

Student: I'm only fourteen, Miss P. As of right now, my life plan is just to get to heaven.

HOW THEY TURN OUT

It was quickly becoming a trend in my young life that I would teach Monday through Friday while also juggling youth ministry responsibilities in a parish with speaking gigs bookending my week. It was just another weekend and another airplane when I was settling into seat 9A, headphones plugged into my iPad and a nap my number one priority, when the middle-aged gentleman sitting in 9B tapped me on the shoulder and pleasantly asked, "Are you traveling for work or pleasure?"

My mom always told me that I have a "conversational face," the type that didn't have a sour expression plastered across it, which meant I should be prepared for people to always want to visit with me. Being an introvert through and through, I hate this feature about myself because in whatever twistedly funny cosmos God is running, it means I always get stuck talking to people on airplanes.

"Work," I replied, hoping my one word answer would deter him from continued chatting.

"Oh, what do you do?" he quickly asked.

"I'm a teacher and youth minister," I said. I was convinced short answers would quickly end the conversation.

"My mother was a teacher," the man said. "She taught for fifty-one years. Eighth-grade English. That woman could diagram a sentence in ten seconds flat."

I nodded and smiled in my seat as I slowly lifted the right ear bud closer to my face, hoping he'd get the hint that I desperately wanted to stop talking.

"You know, I could never be a teacher; you know why?" He leaned in close, a big smile crossing his face. "My mom used to say being a teacher was the hardest job in the world, not because the pay was low or the kids were bad but because at the end of the school year you'd have to say goodbye and you never knew how they would turn out."

He turned back to his magazine, and I put my headphones in. The conversation was now over, right at the moment my mind went into overdrive.

He was right! Teachers do put in a whole lot of effort. Endless hours, piles of grading, ceaseless disciplining, never-ending lesson planning, and anxious worrying over the course of nine months ends with a swift, "Have a good summer (i.e., good riddance!)" as they walk out the door for the last time and head off to the great, big world (or just to tenth grade). Time, energy, talent, and treasure is poured into the formation of the hearts, minds, and souls of my students, and the likelihood of me ever seeing the effects of my effort is slim to none. They'll go through the rest of high school and may never think twice about Room 24. They'll head off to college and graduate, get married and start having kids of their own, and the diagram of the Trinity and the organization of the seven sacraments won't ever cross their minds. I will be forgotten, my jokes will be misremembered and poorly told, and the concepts taught will probably become fuzzy.

The gentleman in seat 9B was right: I would probably never know how most of the students I taught would turn out. But what he didn't realize was that I, a mere classroom evangelist in small, windowless, cluttered Room 24 in Lake Charles, Louisiana, didn't necessarily need to know. All that mattered, in the end, was that I did my best to help them achieve the greatest and most important task of their lives: to become saints.

REAL FAILURE

I have always despised assigning saint projects, mostly because it means that I have to sit through dozens of presentations on the same greatest hits list of holy men and women time after time. There are sure to be at least a dozen St. Augustines and Mother Teresas, with an equal number of St. Francises of Assisi and St. Thérèses of Lisieux. The same Wikipedia article is cited, the same few pictures are on the PowerPoint slides, and the same stories about the life of the saint are recounted. So after a painful go of it in my first year of teaching, I wised up in my second year and decided to give them a list from which to choose with no repeats allowed.

Two weeks later, after conducting research at the library and writing a three-page paper on their chosen saint, students had to give a brief presentation on the saint they chose. It took nearly a week to get through all the presentations, each one more similar than the last, despite the variety of saints studied. It slowly became obvious to me that in the end, all saints had the same theme to their lives: love God, do good things for him, bring people closer to Jesus.

On Friday, with just a few presentations to go, another student took to the front of the room to give his report on St. Maximilian Kolbe. To be entirely honest, I was only half listening through most of the student's report. I could see he had done a good deal of research and knew the stories of Maximilian's life, so when he reached the final slide I was in the midst of writing "A+, good work" on the rubric and attaching a gold star to the top.

"You know, when I was researching the life of St. Maximilian Kolbe, one thought kept coming into my mind, Miss Prejean." My head popped up. I hadn't realized the student had gone "off book" and wasn't following the bullet points on his slides anymore.

"All I could keep thinking was that Maximilian Kolbe's life ended in tragedy. He was in a concentration camp dying in place of another person. That's tragic. He was being starved to death. That's pretty tragic. He had to be killed with a lethal injection. That's the worst thing I've ever heard. So, you know what I did, Miss Prejean? I googled the words 'saint' and 'tragedy' to try and find something that could help me make sense of it all. And I found this."

The student clicked to the final slide, and projected onto the screen was a quote from Léon Bloy, a French novelist who converted to Catholicism in youth after encountering a few holy men and women while working in Paris: "The only real sadness, the only real failure, the only great tragedy in life is not to become a saint."

Silence filled the classroom before my student concluded his presentation by saying, "I think St. Maximilian Kolbe avoided that great tragedy, Miss Prejean. Hopefully we'll all avoid it too."

EVANGELIZE WELL

My freshman year of college, I became friends with Fr. J.D., an old Dominican friar who served as the campus chaplain. He was well over six-feet five-inches tall with a penchant for wearing the same faded white habit every day that had a slightly moldy smell. At the end of every Mass, right before giving us the final blessing, he'd look out in the congregation and say, "Study well, students. Study well." It was never "study hard" or "study a lot" but always "study well," reminding us that doing one hour of one thing with great effort was far better than attempting to do a lot of things over the course of many hours poorly. Perhaps the same principle can be applied to our efforts in evangelization.

The most essential elements of evangelization include the joyful extension of invitations that promote and foster prayerful encounters with Christ, which then lead to the building of relationships that include open, honest, humble dialogue about the Truth. In short: joyfully meet people, prayerfully show them Jesus, deeply love them, and then patiently walk with them on their journey, helping them grow in knowledge of the Truth at every step of the way. Most important, do all of this well.

Our world is already overrun with mediocrity. Many people, myself included, sometimes put in the least amount of effort needed to get by. But evangelization has to go beyond the bare minimum. Evangelization is the proclamation of the Truth. It is the sharing of the Gospel. Teaching Jesus to a student, neighbor, coworker, friend, or complete stranger is the most important thing any of us could ever hope to do, and as such, evangelization deserves our very best efforts. Evangelization demands excellence. This requires genuine welcoming as we invite others to a personal encounter with Christ, which then requires us to take the time to engage hard questions, build authentic relationships, and joyfully live in witness to the Truth we share and proclaim. And we do all this not because it builds up ourselves but because it promotes Christ's Kingdom of peace here on earth and helps people find their way to heaven.

This is our first and most essential task that cannot be taken lightly. To do so would be to relegate evangelization to nothing more than an occasional hobby, no different than crocheting blankets or fly fishing in June. Doing evangelization well means that we are committed, beyond all else, to sharing Christ's healing presence with our broken world and helping lead people closer to Christ in this life so that they can be united with him in the next. If we evangelize well, pouring all that we are into our inviting, encountering, and relationship building, then we are doing nothing short of helping people enjoy eternal life with the Lord. There is no better task, no higher calling, no greater purpose in life than to help someone avoid the great tragedy of not becoming a saint. This is why we evangelize. This is why we are evangelized. This is why we go beyond ourselves to invite people to meet and fall in love with Christ and do his work of bringing peace and justice to the world.

We go far beyond simply saying, "I love Jesus and I want you to love him also." We say, not just in our words but by the way we live, "I love Jesus and he has called me to be his hands and feet in this world, to be his witness to others by feeding the hungry and giving drink to the thirsty, by welcoming the stranger and clothing the naked, by caring for the sick and visiting prisoners" (see Mt 25:35). When we evangelize, we call others to mission. When we evangelize, we become missionaries. When we evangelize, we go outside of ourselves to speak Truth, live Truth, and we are privileged to watch the Truth transform the world.

Knowing how great the call to evangelization would be, Jesus gave us the communion of the Church, a body of believers under the inspiration of the Holy Spirit to guide, strengthen, and comfort us along the way. Our work on behalf of justice announces the salvation we know through Christ; our efforts usher people into the community, the family, of the Church. The Church in turn is the soil in which our witness and faith is able to grow, for it is within the Church that we receive the grace we so desperately need.

HOPEFULLY HEAVEN

When I first sat down to write this book, a fear kept creeping into my mind, paralyzing me at times and stopping the writing process in its tracks. "What if I'm wrong?" I kept asking myself. "What if this idea that evangelizing should center around inviting, encountering, and relationship building is just a bunch of fooie? What if it's just nonsense that isn't actually right at all?" Sure, I've learned a lot through my frequent failures and infrequent successes in the classroom, but that doesn't mean that my understanding is necessarily correct . . . it's not like any of my students have been canonized.

And then it hit me: the fruits of what I've done in Room 24 may never be known to me in this life. In fact, the invitations extended, the encounters fostered, and the relationships built have been but a planting of the seed, a seed that I hope will grow into something beautiful and good in the lives of my students. All evangelization, in the end, is a mere chapter in the great book of someone's life, and we are blessed to get to help write even just a few pages.

Less than a month into my teaching career, the same young man that I called insane in the first week raised his hand in class one day. He sarcastically asked, "Miss Prejean, what, in your opinion, is the meaning of life?"

I knew he was trying to do a bait and switch and that whatever answer I gave would certainly not change his mind or fix his disrespectful tone, so I decided to have a bit of fun with my answer.

"Well, first, we have to ask why we exist." I wrote "Why?" on the board followed by an arrow. "The answer is simple," I said. I drew "God's love" after the arrow.

I could see the student rolling his eyes as I continued on. "Then, we have to ask how we exist. That one is easy; it says it right at the beginning of the Bible. We are made in God's image and likeness with the gift of free will." I wrote every-thing out on the board, continuing on with my made-up-on-the-spot diagram.

"Finally, and this is most important to the meaning of life, we need to ask, where are we headed?" At this point I paused. Every student in the room was paying attention except the one that asked, so I zeroed in on him and said very slowly, "We are headed to heaven to become saints." I paused to let the magnitude of what I said sink in before saying with a smile, "Hopefully."

The student rolled his eyes, and said, "Well good luck. I have no intention of going there since it doesn't even exist."

I smiled back at him, heartbroken he was so bitter at such a young age but also excited at the prospect that there was still plenty of time for him to change his mind at some point in the future. I took a deep breath and said, "It's my job to get you to heaven. Challenge accepted."

ACKNOWLEDGMENTS

There are not enough pages in this book that could contain the names and accolades of the countless people who helped make *Room 24* possible. First, thank you to the amazing people at Ave Maria Press, especially the ever kind, diligent, patient, and fun Eileen Ponder. If you hadn't answered my first e-mail, we wouldn't be here, and if you hadn't kept answering the countless e-mails throughout the writing process, this book wouldn't exist. To Christopher Wesley who asked me to write a blurb for his book, which put me in touch with Eileen in the first place, thank you for thinking of me and thank you for being such a fantastic servant of the Lord. To Mike Patin, you have been the best mentor I could have ever hoped for, turning into the finest friend and colleague I never expected to be blessed with. Thank you for all you've done for me, Goose.

Thank you to Tom and Sandy McGrady. You welcomed me into your home and let me set up camp at your dining room table, where the majority of this book was written. I've gained a second family in y'all, and I love you both. To my wonderful coworkers in the vineyard at St. Louis Catholic High School, Our Lady Queen of Heaven Church, and in the Diocese of Lake Charles: your flexibility, support, encouragement, and witness to me is invaluable. To my students who have put up with me in the classroom and let me play a small part in their formation: you are the reason I'm convinced I have even half a shot at getting to heaven, if for no other reason than you show me the face of Christ every day. Thanks for being wonderful and for teaching me more than I could ever teach you. To the men and women who have taught me at Our Lady Queen of Heaven Catholic School, St. Louis Catholic High School, the University of Dallas, and the Augustine Institute: you have been my instructors in so much and my inspiration in so many ways. Without you, I know I would not be a teacher myself.

To Makinzy and Josh Fontenot and my favorite children in the world, Jondavid and Marian: you have been my stress reliefs, sounding boards, reality checks, and dearest friends. To my Grandma Libby and Papa Gus: your quiet support and constant prayers throughout this process were a tremendous comfort. To my little sister, Laura: thank you for reading these pages in their earliest drafts and making me laugh, even when I'm not smart enough to understand your humor.

To my mom and dad, Marie and Garland: I have no doubt I would not be half the person I am today were it not for your parenting. Thanks for always buying me dinner, for reading everything I've ever written, and for listening to everything I've ever said. Thank you for keeping me humble and grounded, never mincing your words for mere comfort. Your honesty is my balance. Most of all, thank for giving me life. It's pretty great and I appreciate it. I love you both. Finally, to the love of my life, Tommy: your ceaseless love, steady support, and boundless energy have kept me going since the very first time we spoke and in every moment thereafter. I love you, and I like you.

KATIE PREJEAN is a passionate teacher, youth minister, author, and speaker who travels across the country using her unique style of "theological comedy" with audiences ranging in size from ten to ten thousand. Her original blend of humor and storytelling—along with her teaching of hard-hitting theological truth—is dynamic, engaging, and challenging. Prejean reads voraciously, blogs occasionally, works out daily, roots for the New Orleans Saints, doesn't like to be hugged, and dances with a vengeance (though not very well). She has her bachelor's degree in theology from the University of Dallas and is working on her masters in theological studies from the Augustine Institute. Prejean is the freshman theology teacher and assistant campus minister at St. Louis Catholic High School and also serves as the youth director at Our Lady Queen of Heaven Church. She lives in Lake Charles, Louisiana, with her dog, Barney.

AVE
AVE MARIA PRESS

Founded in 1865, Ave Maria Press,
a ministry of the Congregation of
Holy Cross, is a Catholic publishing
company that serves the spiritual and
formative needs of the Church and its
schools, institutions, and ministers;
Christian individuals and families; and
others seeking spiritual nourishment.

For a complete listing of titles from

Ave Maria Press

Sorin Books

Forest of Peace

Christian Classics

visit www.avemariapress.com

AVE MARIA PRESS
Notre Dame, IN
A Ministry of the United States Province of Holy Cross